Pronunciation Pairs

Pronunciation Pairs

Teacher's Manual

Ann Baker • Sharon Goldstein

CAMBRIDGE
UNIVERSITY PRESS

PUBLISHED BY THE PRESS SYNDICATE OF THE UNIVERSITY OF CAMBRIDGE
The Pitt Building, Trumpington Street, Cambridge, United Kingdom

CAMBRIDGE UNIVERSITY PRESS
The Edinburgh Building, Cambridge CB2 2RU, UK
40 West 20th Street, New York, NY 10011–4211, USA
10 Stamford Road, Oakleigh, Melbourne 3166, Australia
Ruiz de Alarcón 13, 28014 Madrid, Spain
Dock House, The Waterfront, Cape Town 8001, South Africa

http://www.cambridge.org

First published 1990
8th printing 2000

Printed in the United States of America

Typeset in Sabon

Library of Congress Cataloging-in-Publication Data
Baker, Ann
Pronunciation pairs: an introductory course for students of English /
Ann Baker, Sharon Goldstein.
p. cm.
Teacher's manual.
1. English language – Pronunciation. 2. English language – Textbooks
for foreign speakers. I. Goldstein, Sharon. II. Title.
PE1137.B215   1989
428.3'dc19   89–726
                                                                  CIP

British Library Cataloguing in Publication Data
Baker, Ann
Pronunciation pairs: an introductory course for students of English.
Teacher's book.
1. English language. Pronuncation
I. Title II. Goldstein, Sharon
428.1

ISBN 0-521-34973-7 Teacher's Manual
ISBN 0-521-34972-9 Student's Book
ISBN 0-521-34167-1 Set of 4 Cassettes

Contents

Introduction   1

Overview of the Detailed Teaching Notes   5

Detailed Teaching Notes   13

Section A Vowels   13

Unit 1 iy (sheep)   13
Unit 2 ɪ (ship)   16
Unit 3 ɛ (yes)   18
Unit 4 ey (train)   20
Unit 5 æ (hat)   22
Unit 6 Review   24
Unit 7 ʌ (cup)   25
Unit 8 Part 1 ə (a banana)   27
Unit 8 Part 2 ɔr (letter)   29
Unit 9 ɑ (father)   30
Unit 10 ɔ (ball)   32
Unit 11 ow (no)   34
Unit 12 ʊ (book)   36
Unit 13 uw (boot)   38
Unit 14 Review   40
Unit 15 ay (fine)   41
Unit 16 ɔy (boy)   43
Unit 17 aw (house)   45
Unit 18 Review   46
Unit 19 ə (a camera) Review   47
Unit 20 ɜr (word)   49

Section B Consonants   52

Unit 21 p (pen)   52
Unit 22 b (baby)   54
Unit 23 t (tie)   55
Unit 24 d (door)   58
Unit 25 k (key)   60
Unit 26 g (girl)   62
Unit 27 s (sun)   64
Unit 28 z (zoo)   66
Unit 29 ʃ (shoe)   69
Unit 30 ʒ (television)   70
Unit 31 tʃ (chair)   72
Unit 32 dʒ (joke)   73
Unit 33 f (fan)   75
Unit 34 v (van)   77
Unit 35 w (window)   79
Unit 36 y (yellow)   81
Unit 37 h (hat)   83
Unit 38 θ (think)   85
Unit 39 ð (the feather)   87
Unit 40 m (mouth)   89
Unit 41 n (nose)   91
Unit 42 ŋ (ring)   93
Unit 43 l Part 1 (letter)   95
Unit 44 l Part 2 (ball)   97
Unit 45 r Part 1 (rain)   99
Unit 46 r Part 2 (here)   101

Diagnostic Test   105
List of Likely Errors   108

Pronunciation Pairs

Introduction

The primary objectives of most language learners are to understand and to be understood – to hear and speak the language clearly. Crucial for meeting these objectives is the ability to recognize and pronounce the sounds of the target language. Yet, too often pronunciation practice is not adequately incorporated into the beginning and intermediate levels of language teaching. As a result, mistakes inevitably made in those early stages become "fossilized" – repeated so many times that they become difficult, if not impossible, to eradicate. The long-term answer to this problem of the "fossilized accent" is to begin teaching pronunciation from the beginning stages of language learning and to make it an integral part of course work thereafter. *Pronunciation Pairs* has been developed for just that purpose.

Pronunciation Pairs is a comprehensive pronunciation course for English learners at the elementary through intermediate levels – when pronunciation practice is likely to do the most good. Its primary focus is on teaching sounds – not only the individual sounds, but also the stress and intonation patterns of English. Through a wide variety of interesting, lively, and amusing exercises and activities, *Pronunciation Pairs* provides pronunciation practice that is communicatively valuable and that can be linked to other course work. Accompanying Cassettes contain the practice material, recorded in a variety of voices. The Teacher's Manual provides teachers with suggestions for lesson procedures, detailed notes on each unit in the Student's Book, ideas for further practice and for linking the material to other course work, as well as guidance in selecting material relevant to students' particular needs.

Selecting material appropriate to the students

Students with different native languages have different pronunciation problems. Particularly at beginning levels, some students may be happy to spend time on sounds that are easy for them, relieved to find an English sound that they can pronounce. But time is usually precious, and teachers should be aware of how relevant practice is to students' real pronunciation needs. The Diagnostic Test on page 105 of the Teacher's Manual can be used to determine the pronunciation problems of particular language groups or to identify the errors made by individual students. This test can be photocopied for class distribution. The List of Likely Errors on pages 108 – 129 of the Teacher's Manual gives information on the difficulties speakers of different languages are likely to have. In the Detailed Teaching Notes for each unit, the section headed "Student Difficulties" gives information on which language groups can be expected to have difficulty with the sound practiced, providing teachers with an indication of how relevant each unit is to the students.

Organization of the Student's Book

Pronunciation Pairs is divided into two sections – one on vowels and one on consonants. Each section begins with an introductory unit familiarizing students with the basic mouth positions and movements they will need to use in producing the sounds of English. Following these brief introductions are the units (twenty in the vowel section and twenty-six in the consonant section), each teaching a specific sound or (in the section on vowels) reviewing a group of sounds previously introduced. Each unit follows the general format described in the following paragraphs.

Mouth illustrations and sound production notes

When learning a language, students often have difficulty hearing unfamiliar sounds or hearing the differences between some sounds. It helps to *show* students how sounds are produced. Each unit of *Pronunciation Pairs* begins with an illustration that shows the positions of the mouth and tongue for producing the sound being practiced. Notes that accompany each illustration explain how to make the sound. Together with the Cassette recording (or with the teacher modeling the sound), these materials will help the students understand how the sound is produced.

Sound contrast pairs

Illustrated pairs of words that show a sound contrast appear in nearly every unit. Each set of pairs contrasts two sounds that students often confuse. (Use the Student Difficulties section in each unit of the Detailed Teaching Notes to help determine which sounds students of particular language backgrounds are likely to confuse.) Often students learning a language have difficulty with the sounds of the new language, hearing a new sound as being more like a sound in their own language or hearing two different sounds in the new language as the same. Practice with the sound contrast pairs helps students learn to recognize and produce the target sound in each unit and to distinguish it from other sounds in English with which it might be confused.

Illustrations of the sound contrast pairs help students understand what they are practicing. When it is made visually obvious that there is a difference between *ship* and *sheep* – that altering a single sound in a word can change its meaning completely – students are better motivated to practice, since they are made to see the importance of correct pronunciation for communication.

Vocabulary has been limited as much as possible. More difficult words have been included when necessary, particularly in the illustrated lists, but an attempt has been made throughout to use only simple, everyday words.

Sentence recognition tests

Every unit in which a sound contrast has been introduced also contains a sentence recognition test – a series of sentences offering a choice of words with the sound contrast. Students listen to the sentences and identify which of the words is said. This gives the students practice in hearing the target sound in connected speech and tests their ability to distinguish between the sound contrasts within the context of a sentence.

Word practice lists

Each unit of the Student's Book provides lists of words containing the sound being practiced, usually taken from the dialogue or the exercises that follow. These lists are not illustrated, except in the few lessons where illustrated word lists replace the sound contrast practice.

Dialogues/conversations/games

Each unit of the Student's Book contains a dialogue or other reading material, along with pair work or other group practice material. This material, which is lively and frequently humorous, contains a high concentration of the sound (or sounds) being practiced. Work on pronunciation calls for extended practice, and students are more highly motivated to listen to, repeat, and even learn dialogues or other contextualized practice material than they are to practice isolated or meaningless sentences.

Stress and intonation

Even though some students can pronounce and recognize every English sound, their speech still may be unintelligible and they may be unable to understand the spoken language if they have not mastered English stress and intonation patterns. These patterns are important factors for communicating in English. In almost every unit some aspect of stress and/or intonation is introduced and practiced. Additional material for word stress practice is provided in the Detailed Teaching Notes in the Teacher's Manual.

In sections practicing stress or intonation, stressed syllables are shown in darker, boldfaced type. Arrows indicating the direction (rising or falling) of the intonation are shown over the parts of a sentence where there is a change in intonation.

Linking pronunciation and spelling

Students are very often puzzled by English spelling. It may seem to them to be not only arbitrary but also unrelated to any other part of their course. Linking spelling and pronunciation provides a systematic approach to the teaching of spelling, as well as an opportunity for further practice and review of pronunciation material. Each unit of the Student's Book concludes with a spelling section that lists basic spelling patterns for the sound being practiced. These spelling lists use words taught in the unit as examples, as well as other words that illustrate the patterns.

Using the Cassette recordings

A Cassette symbol ▭ is used in the Student's Book to indicate all material recorded on the accompanying set of Cassettes. For each unit this material includes the instructions for producing the sound, sound contrast practice, sentence recognition test, word practice list, dialogue (or other reading material), and examples of the stress or intonation pattern practiced. Although teachers can use the text without using the Cassettes, the recordings will give students the opportunity to hear a wider range of voices and pronunciation models. Perhaps most important, students can use the Cassettes on their own or in a language laboratory, listening to the material as many times as they find necessary. Repeated listening practice and self-monitoring is often crucial for improving pronunciation.

Connecting pronunciation to other course work

Teachers often find that students can master a pronunciation problem in pronunciation lessons but inevitably lapse in general class work or in ordinary speech. The answer to this problem is not to abandon teaching pronunciation but to tie it in with general language teaching as much as possible. For example, if students have difficulty with the sound /ʃ/, it can be practiced in lessons on:
1. describing actions using *she* ("She's reading.")
2. talking about nationality ("What nationality is she? Is she Polish?")
3. asking for advice ("What should I write?")

A particular lesson should not be exclusively "pronunciation" or "course work," but instead should be a combination. Few pronunciation difficulties will be overcome with one isolated pronunciation lesson. The teacher should be prepared for a very slow process in which the problem is approached in as many different contexts, on as many different occasions, and using as many different materials as possible.

The Detailed Teaching Notes that follow provide suggestions for linking the teaching of pronunciation with other course work. These suggestions are found under the headings "Linking pronunciation with other course work" and "Further practice."

Overview of the Detailed Teaching Notes

The Detailed Teaching Notes present teaching procedures for each unit in the Student's Book as well as suggestions for further practice and for linking the material to other course work. The detailed notes for each unit follow the general organization described in the following sections and frequently refer back to this overview.

Sound production

Instructions on how to produce the sound being practiced appear at the beginning of each unit in the Student's Book. Make sure that students understand how the sound in each unit is made. Demonstrate where possible and model the sound. Students should watch your mouth as you make the sound. Use the Cassettes as an additional model. For many sounds, it is also helpful for students to use small hand mirrors to watch their own mouths as they say the sound. The Detailed Teaching Notes for each unit include amplified instructions or additional notes on some sounds; these can be read or paraphrased to the class according to the teacher's discretion.

Students briefly practice the sound in isolation. Even with a large class, it should be possible to check every student's performance at this stage. The teacher can give further individual help to those who need it during the group practice later on. Do not dwell too long on the production of individual sounds: Students may become discouraged if they are expected to pronounce isolated sounds perfectly. Note, too, that sounds become modified in the stream of speech, as they occur surrounded by other sounds. Sounds pronounced in isolation often have an artificial quality.

Variation

The Detailed Teaching Notes frequently include a section on variation to point out different ways the sound may be produced by different speakers of English or in different contexts. These sections are included for reference, to be discussed with students at the discretion of the teacher, according to the level of the class and the relevance of the note to the particular students.

Student difficulties

This section of the Detailed Teaching Notes gives information on the difficulties students with different native languages are likely to encounter in each unit, often with suggestions for dealing with particular problems. A summary of common errors made by speakers of different languages appears in an index (the List of Likely Errors) at the back of the Teacher's Manual. For more details on the pronunciation problems of various nationalities, teachers may find it useful to consult

Learner English (Cambridge University Press, 1987) or a contrastive analysis of the language in question.

Suggested procedures

This section of the Detailed Teaching Notes contains information on specific language items and suggested procedures for using the material in each unit of the Student's Book. The suggested procedures are merely that – suggestions. The teaching procedures actually used will vary according to the students' level and the teachers' own methods.

Sound contrast pairs

Check that students understand the vocabulary in the illustrated sound contrast pairs at the beginning of the unit. Where necessary, demonstrate the meaning of the word, or use the word in a sentence suitable to the class level. Students should listen to the Cassette or to the teacher and repeat the words, reading from the list first vertically and then horizontally. If possible, students should cover the words, with initial practice done using the pictures only.

Example: Sound 1   Sound 2
             sheep   ship
             heel   hill
             seat   sit

Practice in this order:
  a. sheep, heel, seat
  b. ship, hill, sit
  c. sheep/ship, heel/hill, seat/sit

This practice is recorded on the Cassette for each unit. If you model the words yourself rather than use the Cassette, try to keep the intonation the same for both words in a pair to avoid confusing students (especially students who speak tone languages like Chinese, in which pitch is part of the pronunciation of a word).

Recognition practice   It is suggested that teachers occasionally vary the lessons to avoid monotony, selecting from among the following procedures for sound contrast practice. This part of the lesson should be done at a fairly brisk pace, and students should be given immediate feedback as to whether their responses are correct or not.

1. The teacher reads two words from the list of sound contrast pairs. Students say whether the words were the same or different (for example, by responding orally or by writing "S" or "D").
Example: TEACHER: Sheep. Ship.
             STUDENTS: Different.
             TEACHER: Seat. Seat.
             STUDENTS: Same.

2. The teacher reads words at random from the list of sound contrast pairs. Students indicate if they heard sound 1 or sound 2 (for example, by saying the numbers or by holding up one or two fingers).

Example: TEACHER: Hill.
            STUDENTS: 2.
            TEACHER: Seat.
            STUDENTS: 1.

3. The teacher points to a picture and says one of the words in the sound contrast pairs. Students say whether the word was the correct one.
Example: TEACHER: (*pointing to picture of sheep*) Ship.
            STUDENTS: Wrong (*or* No).
            TEACHER: (*pointing to picture of hill*) Hill.
            STUDENTS: Right (*or* Yes).

4. The teacher says one of the words in a pair. Students choose between paraphrases (for example, written on the blackboard or on a paper handout).
Example: TEACHER: Ship.
            STUDENTS: A boat.
            TEACHER: Sheep.
            STUDENTS: An animal.

5. The teacher introduces new words. These could be taken from the list of words for further practice in the Detailed Teaching Notes for that unit, although it is not necessary to use words that are part of sound contrast pairs. Students say whether the word contained sound 1 or sound 2.
Example: TEACHER: Big.
            STUDENTS: 2.
            TEACHER: Little.
            STUDENTS: 2.
            TEACHER: Leave.
            STUDENTS: 1.

6. The teacher says three words, two of which are the same. Students identify the word that was different.
Example: TEACHER: (One) sheep; (two) ship; (three) ship.
            STUDENTS: (One) sheep.
After initial practice, individual students can take the part of the teacher in any of these procedures.

Further examples of sound contrast pairs are given in the Detailed Teaching Notes for each unit. Sometimes these examples include words from a more advanced vocabulary than the words generally used in the Student's Book. Teachers should base their decision as to whether to use these further examples on the students' level and need for further practice and on their own ability to illustrate, explain, or translate the words given.

Sentence recognition test

Students look at the sentences in their books and then circle the word in parentheses that they hear in each sentence as it is read by the teacher or played on the Cassette. The answers are given in the Detailed Teaching Notes for each unit.

These sentences can also be used for practice, adapting procedures described for sound contrast pairs. For example:

1. The teacher says a sentence. Students choose between meaningful responses or paraphrases.
Example: TEACHER: She isn't going to live.
            STUDENTS: She's going to die.
            TEACHER: She isn't going to leave.
            STUDENTS: She's going to stay.
Students can also practice like this in pairs.

2. The teacher points to a picture, and says one of the sentences. Students say whether the sentence was correct or not, adding the correct sentence if the original one was wrong.
            TEACHER: *(pointing to picture of ship)* Columbus went to America on
                         a sheep.
            STUDENTS: He went to America on a ship.

Word practice lists

Each unit of the Student's Book provides additional practice lists of words containing the sound being taught, usually taken from the dialogue and containing the sound being taught. Students listen to and repeat each word in the list as it is pronounced on the Cassette or by the teacher. The words can be practiced either before or after students listen to the dialogue. Play the Cassette, pausing after each word, or read the words yourself, reading the columns vertically (except the illustrated lists, which are read horizontally). Students repeat chorally. A few individual students could be asked to repeat difficult words. If additional practice is needed, read words at random from the list; have students repeat them. To vary the procedure, read words within each column in mixed order; have students listen and repeat them.

Discuss any unfamiliar vocabulary that is essential for understanding the dialogue that follows. You may prefer, however, to let students listen to the dialogue before discussing vocabulary so that they will hear the words in context.

Dialogue

The dialogues provide concentrated, contextualized practice of the target sound in each unit.

Procedures   Introduce the dialogue, either by briefly describing the setting and the characters or by giving students a listening goal. For example, write one or more questions on the blackboard about information contained in the dialogue; students listen for the answers as they listen to the dialogue. Occasionally, you may want to ask students to listen for a particular linguistic feature (such as a sound or a grammatical form they have been working on) as the listening goal, with students signaling as they hear the item.

Listening   Students close their books or cover the dialogue. Tell them that they will hear the dialogue twice and that the second time they will be able to read along. Play the Cassette. Students answer any questions given (as described above). Play the Cassette again. This time students follow along in their books. Discuss new vocabulary or any difficulties students have.

To vary the procedure, you could prepare a handout or a transparency on an overhead projector with the dialogue presented as a cloze, with blanks replacing some of the words (for example, every fifth word, or words likely to cause difficulty). Students fill in the blanks as they listen to the dialogue and then check their answers against the original dialogue in their books.

Additional practice   Although most of the dialogues are intended primarily for practice in listening to the target sound in context, they can also be used for extra oral practice. Longer dialogues or lines from dialogues can be shortened for student practice, according to the class level.

Possible procedure: Read the dialogue aloud or play the Cassette, pausing after each sentence. Students repeat chorally. If students have difficulty, especially in saying a line smoothly or with the right rhythm, try using "backward buildup." With this technique, sentences are broken down into words and increasingly larger phrases, working from the end of the sentence backward. Students repeat each segment after the teacher. For example:

My eyes are closed and I'm going back to sleep.
to sleep
back to sleep
going back to sleep
and I'm going back to sleep
etc.

When students practice the dialogue, encourage them to look up as they say each line, rather than looking down at their books. Students should read each line (or phrase, if the line is long) silently and then look up as they say the line. Demonstrate this to students. This "read and look up" procedure helps students to group words into phrases said with natural intonation rather than read word by word. Depending on student interest, dialogues could also be practiced in groups, with the teacher moving around the room checking pronunciation and students taking turns at different roles. However, before spending a great deal of time on practicing the dialogue at this point, keep in mind that most units contain guided pronunciation practice later in the lesson, often based on the dialogue.

Stress/intonation

Students listen to and repeat the examples of the stress or intonation pattern being practiced. (The examples are recorded on the Cassette.) If necessary, teachers should supplement these with further examples from the unit or other material familiar to students. Discussion of the stress or intonation pattern practiced, including a description of likely student difficulties and suggested teaching procedures, appears in the Detailed Teaching Notes for each unit. More general information on English stress, rhythm, and intonation can also be found in the Detailed Teaching Notes for Units 8, 16, and 19.

Stress   In English, stress plays a major role in showing which words in a sentence are important. Only the important words in a sentence (usually "content" words like nouns, verbs, adjectives, and adverbs) are stressed. The unimportant words (usually "grammatical" words like prepositions, articles, conjunctions, and auxiliary verbs) are unstressed. Syllables that are stressed are generally pronounced in English with more force, with a longer vowel, and often with a higher pitch than unstressed syllables.

If students have difficulty with the stress in a sentence (for example, if they stress too many words), it may help to write the sentence on the blackboard, showing the stressed words in capital letters and writing the other words very small. Or, draw variously sized dots on the blackboard to represent the rhythm of the sentence: large dark dots for stressed syllables, small light dots for unstressed syllables. Tap with a ruler or clap to demonstrate the stress and rhythm of a sentence. Students can then tap on their desks or clap as you say the sentence and they repeat it.

Intonation   Intonation is the pattern of the voice as it rises and falls in speaking. It is very important in expressing meaning (for example, in showing what kind of sentence – statement, yes/no question, exclamation, etc. – is being said) and in expressing feelings or attitudes (such as surprise, irony, annoyance, enthusiasm).

Use hand gestures or arrows drawn on the blackboard to show the direction of the intonation or to correct errors. If students have difficulty at first, check to make sure they understand the distinction between rising and falling intonation. Draw two arrows on the blackboard: ↗ ↘. Label the arrows "rising" and "falling." Say words or students' names, varying your intonation ("Coffee?" "Tomorrow." "Maria?"). As you say each one, students indicate whether the intonation was rising or falling.

Conversation/game/other group work

In most lessons, the final activity in the Student's Book is a guided conversation or some other group work designed so that students practice both the sound and the stress/intonation pattern introduced in the unit. First make sure that students know what to do by going over a few examples with the whole class listening.

While the students are involved in group work, the teacher should be free to give further individual help to those who need it. During the time spent on group work, students could be asked to act out parts of the dialogue in addition to doing the activity suggested in this section.

Spelling

It is suggested that the spelling material at the end of each unit in the Student's Book be left until the rest of the unit has been completed and be introduced in a later lesson. In the initial practice of a new sound, the spelling of words very often distracts students from the correct pronunciation rather than helps them. The spelling sections provide an opportunity for further practice and review of the words presented in the unit. Additional words, not taken from the unit, are often included to illustrate a spelling pattern, for practice according to the level of the class. Teachers may want to add or substitute other words familiar to students.

The simplest way of introducing the spelling material is to ask students, for example, "How do you write/spell the sound iy?" and to build up a blackboard summary of lists of words for each spelling of the sound, using students' suggestions whenever possible. Add spellings that students miss, underlining the spelling that represents the sound in an example word. Ask a student to try pronouncing the word, or say the word and have students repeat it. Call attention to generalizations that can be made about a particular spelling pattern (e.g., that it only occurs at the end of a word). The Detailed Teaching Notes often give suggestions for further practice of the spelling patterns, such as practice in distinguishing between similar spellings used for different sounds.

Further practice

This section in the Detailed Teaching Notes provides teaching material for further practice if needed. This may involve further practice of the sound, the stress or intonation pattern taught in the unit, or a related feature of pronunciation. In some units, this section ties pronunciation in with another aspect of course work, and teachers may wish to use the material in another lesson.

Linking pronunciation with other course work

This section of the Detailed Teaching Notes contains some specific suggestions for linking the material in each unit of the Student's Book to other course work. For some units, the link is made with teaching a specific grammatical structure; for example, in Unit 42 the sound ŋ is linked with teaching the present continuous tense ("What are they doing?"). For other units the link is more functional; for example, in Unit 13 the sound uw is linked with practice in introducing people ("Nice to meet you, too").

In some cases specific ideas are given for practicing the sound in the suggested context. In other cases, only the context is mentioned; teachers should teach the grammatical structure or other item in whatever way they would normally teach it, but with attention given to the sound in question. Only a few suggestions for practice are made for each unit, and obviously these will not fit in with every course plan. They are merely sample ideas, and teachers should look for other opportunities to tie in their own general course work with teaching pronunciation.

Word stress practice

This section of the Detailed Teaching Notes practices stress in words from the unit being taught (occasionally it also includes words from other units). The format varies, though often the material is presented in the form of a recognition test. Stress patterns are illustrated with dots of varying sizes (e.g., the dots • ● represent the stress pattern in *today*). It is suggested that students practice the stress patterns before taking the test.

Suggested procedures

1. Draw one of the stress patterns shown in the Detailed Teaching Notes on the blackboard, making larger and darker dots to represent stressed syllables and

smaller and lighter dots to represent unstressed syllables. (Sometimes three kinds of dots will be needed, for words that have a lightly stressed syllable.) Tap out the stress pattern with a ruler or pencil and/or show the pattern by clapping. Students should join in.

Example: (*on blackboard*):   ● •

2. Read aloud the words that have this stress pattern. Students listen and repeat the words to the accompaniment of tapping or clapping. Whenever possible, include other words with this stress pattern from the students' known vocabulary.

Example: TEACHER: **Cof**fee, **sand**wich, **Pe**ter, etc.
          STUDENTS: (*listen and repeat*)

3. Write the words on the blackboard and repeat step 2.

4. Students read the words from the blackboard.

5. Repeat steps 1 through 4 for the other stress pattern(s) shown.

6. Recognition Test: Erase all material from the blackboard except the stress pattern dots labeled A, B, and so forth, as in the Detailed Teaching Notes. Students write the numbers 1 through 10 in their notebooks, then listen to the teacher read each item from the list in the teaching notes. Students write the letter that represents the pattern they heard.

Example: (*on blackboard*):   A ● •   B • ●
          TEACHER: Today.
          STUDENTS: B.
          TEACHER: April.
          STUDENTS: A.

Detailed Teaching Notes

Section A   Vowels

The introductory chapter of the Student's Book presents the vocabulary and structures that students will need in order to follow the sound production notes in the units on vowels. The chapter also familiarizes students with some of the basic mouth positions and movements they will use to produce the vowel sounds of English, and helps make them aware of how they use their mouths in producing sounds.

Work through the chapter with the students. It would be helpful for students to use mirrors so that they can watch their own mouths. Students first practice the basic movements of the mouth and tongue. Under the section "Moving your tongue," they practice the positions for producing the sounds iy, ɑ, and uw. These three basic vowels occur in virtually all languages. Becoming aware of how the mouth and tongue move in producing these sounds should make it easier for students to focus on the subtler movements they will need to make in producing other vowel sounds.

Have students practice saying "iy – ɑ – uw" slowly, making the sounds long. Model this, telling students to watch your mouth as you say the sounds. Have students practice saying the sounds several times, focusing on the way their mouths and tongues move as they say these sounds. In the last section of the chapter, students practice tensing their mouth muscles and then relaxing them, as they pronounce a tense vowel (iy) and then a relaxed vowel (ʌ). The distinction between tense and relaxed (or lax) vowels is crucial for distinguishing pairs of vowels like iy/ɪ, ey/ɛ, and uw/ʊ, which students often confuse. If they have difficulty feeling the change in their mouth muscles, have students tighten

and relax other muscles (have them, for example, clench and unclench their fists) as they practice the sounds in the book.

UNIT 1   iy (sheep)

Sound production

See Overview, page 5.

Variation   Length: iy is longest when it is stressed and at the end of a word (as in *tea*) or followed by a voiced consonant (as in *cheese*). It is shorter before voiceless consonants (as in *sheep*). (*Note:* This note on length applies to all vowels.)

Some people pronounce unstressed final -*y*, -*ey*, -*ee*, -*ie*, or -*i* (as in *city, money, coffee, movie,* or *taxi*) as iy; others pronounce it as ɪ. Many people use a sound somewhere between the two – a sound like a short iy.

Student difficulties   Most students do not have trouble producing a sound close to iy. In many languages, such as French, Greek, Hebrew, Japanese, Russian, and Spanish, the sound that resembles English iy is a shorter, "pure" vowel. Students who speak these languages may substitute this shorter sound for iy in English and/or may confuse iy with ɪ. They may need help in learning to pronounce iy as longer and slightly "diphthongized" – that is, pronounced with an extra, short "glide" sound at the end, produced as the tongue glides up from i to y – rather than as the pure vowel i they may be accustomed to from their own languages.

13

Have students first practice the sound iy in places where it is longer and the extra glide sound is more noticeable – in stressed syllables, either alone or before a voiced consonant, as in *tea, see, please, leave, need*. They should feel the tongue move up slightly for the second, glide part of the vowel. If students do not make the vowel long enough, it may be helpful to tell them to say it twice. Note that before a voiceless consonant the glide will be much less noticeable and the vowel will be shorter: compare *need/neat, feed/feet, peas/piece, leave/leaf*. In an unstressed syllable, there may be no glide at all.

For students who do not have trouble with iy, this unit can be used simply to introduce the sound iy for contrastive work in the next unit with ɪ, which most students do find difficult.

Note on vowels: Speakers of some languages, including Arabic and Thai, have a strong tendency to put a glottal stop before all vowels at the beginning of words.

Suggested procedures

Practice 1 and 2   See Overview, page 8.
Other words from the dialogue with the sound iy:
we'd (Unstressed *we'd* may have a vowel closer to
   ɪ than to iy.)
the (*The* may have the sound iy before a vowel, as
   in *the order.*)

Dialogue   See Overview, pages 8–9.
Introduce the situation. Peter, Lee, and Steve are in a restaurant. They are about to order lunch. After students listen to the dialogue, ask a few questions that elicit answers using the sound iy. For example:
How much is the lunch special?
What is Peter having to eat?
Why doesn't Steve want a roast beef sandwich?
Who wants coffee?

Intonation   In this section, students practice intonation in alternative questions – questions that offer a choice between things. Questions with *or* are not always alternative questions; sometimes they can be yes/no questions. The dif-

ference is expressed by intonation. Yes/no questions have rising intonation at the end (only):

Would you like coffee or tea? (= Would you like something to drink?)

In alternative questions, the voice falls on the last choice offered. The voice usually rises on all the choices before the last one:

Would you like coffee or tea?

Students listen to and repeat the examples of alternative questions in the Student's Book (these are recorded on the Cassette). Show the direction of the intonation with hand gestures. Model the example. Ask a student, "Would you like bean soup or pea soup?" The student should answer, choosing one alternative. Have two other students ask and answer an alternative question using the menu. Then students practice in pairs. As they practice, move around the room checking pronunciation. After one student in each pair asks a few questions, the students should reverse roles.

Note:

1. Some students tend to put too much stress on the word *please*.

2. The pronunciation of *would you like* is difficult for some students, who may tend to drop the sound d in *would*. Note that in relaxed conversation native English speakers often pronounce *would you* as wʊdʒə.

Conversation   In small groups of about four people, students role-play ordering food in a restaurant. If possible, rearrange tables and chairs to create a more realistic setting. Students may want to add other phrases commonly used in restaurants ("Are you ready to order?" "Yes. I'll have/I'd like . . ." or "No, not yet/not quite." "Anything else?"). You may also want to discuss other ways of responding to alternative questions (e.g., "Would you like coffee or tea?" "Neither, thank you./Could I have a soda instead?").

Alternative presentation   After students have practiced the sound ɪ in Unit 2, use this conversation activity to review alternative question intonation and the sounds iy and ɪ. Write "Sound 1 (iy)" and "Sound 2 (ɪ)" on the blackboard, and say the sounds. Say the names of foods; students tell you which sound to write them under. Foods with the sound ɪ include fish, chicken, shrimp, liver, spinach, grilled cheese sandwich, vanilla, and milk. Then proceed as above.

Spelling   The many different spellings for the sound iy may be confusing to students, especially those who speak languages in which spelling is regular and more or less phonetic (with a single spelling representing a single sound). Point out that even though there are many English spellings for the sound iy, almost all contain the letter *e*. In English, unlike other languages, the letter *i* does not usually represent the sound iy, except in a few words, such as *ski, visa,* and *police.*

Further practice

Oral spelling   Many students, even fairly advanced ones, have trouble spelling words aloud or understanding oral spellings. They are particularly likely to confuse the letters *e* and *a* or *e* and *i* or to mispronounce the names of consonant letters that use these vowel sounds (e.g., pronouncing *k* as kɑ). The names of nine letters of the alphabet (*b, c, d, e, g, p, t, v,* and *z*) use the iy sound in American English (*z* = ziy in American English, zɛd in British English). Students may mispronounce these letters even if they do not have trouble with the sound iy. (The ey sound of the letter *a* occurs in *a, h, j,* and *k,* and the ay sound occurs in *i* and *y.*)
   Write these letters on the blackboard:
   b c d e g p t v z
Ask students to say the letters. Then give them a list of words, either on the blackboard or on a paper handout. For example:

repeat | chicken
cheese | orange juice
eighteen | believe
zero | *your first and last names*
sandwich | *the name of the person on your right*

Ask students to spell the words aloud. You may

want to have a student write the words on the blackboard as others spell them aloud.

Extension:

1. If students have difficulty with these letters, divide the class into two teams for a spelling competition, with students recording scores on the blackboard. Each student takes a turn to ask a member of the other team to spell a word from this list or from another list that you have prepared.

2. Dictate the spellings of words that might cause confusion (e.g., words with the letters *a, e, i, g,* and *j*).

3. Prepare a short list of words. Divide the class into pairs, giving one student in each pair a copy of the list. That student spells the words aloud; the other student writes them down. Students compare the two lists at the end.

Linking pronunciation with other course work

Tie pronunciation in with practice of:

1. Shopping requests. For example, write on the blackboard:

I'd like	a pound		cheese	peas	please.
Could I have	three pounds	of	veal	leeks	please?
	half a pound		beef	beans	
			coffee	peaches	

Students role-play shopping. Each customer requests two to four items; the store clerk repeats the names of the items. Or, students role-play asking a favor, using a similar blackboard chart:
   I'm going to the store. Do you need anything?
   Yes. Could you get me . . .
One student requests items, which the other student should be able to repeat.

2. Nationalities/languages, such as those ending in *-ese*:
  He's Japanese./She's Portuguese.
  Do you speak Chinese/Greek/Norwegian/
  Swedish/Vietnamese?

Word stress practice

See Overview, pages 11–12.
- • coffee, sandwich, Peter, ice cream, waiter, order, peaches, menu, practice, questions
- •• vegetable, sandwiches, dialogue, alphabet

UNIT 2 ɪ (ship)

Sound production

See Overview, page 5.
  Note: The tongue is a little lower in the mouth for the sound ɪ than for iy. Students should not move their tongues up toward y when saying ɪ.

Variation   Length: ɪ is longest when it is stressed and followed by a voiced consonant. It is shorter before a voiceless consonant. Compare *hid/hit, rib/rip, ridge/rich, his/hiss, Ms./Miss.*
  Unstressed ɪ: In many unstressed syllables, the pronunciation of the vowel may vary between ɪ and ə (as in the third syllable of *American* or in the second syllable of *village*) or between ɪ and iy (as in the second syllable of *city* or *money* or in the first syllable of *because* or *repeat*).

Student difficulties   Nearly all students have difficulty with the sound ɪ. Usually they confuse it with iy, since many languages have only one vowel in the area of iy and ɪ. Arabic students may also confuse it with ɛ. Unfortunately, many pairs of words – and possible sentences – in English are distinguished only by whether they contain the sound iy or the sound ɪ. In some words, students can make embarrassing mistakes if they do not pronounce the vowel correctly (for example, if they do not pronounce the vowels in *beach* and *sheet* clearly as iy rather than ɪ).

When practicing the sounds iy and ɪ in isolation, knowing that ɪ is a much shorter, quieter sound than iy seems to help students. It may also help them to know that ɪ is a much more relaxed sound than iy. By placing their fingers under their chins, they should be able to feel the tension of their muscles when saying iy and the lack of tension in their muscles when saying ɪ. They can use a mirror to check the position of their lips.

Suggested procedures

Practice 1   See Overview, pages 6–7.
  Contrasts for further practice: leave/live, sleep/slip, eat/it, bean/bin, seat/sit, cheap/chip, meal/mill, reach/rich, green/grin, feet/fit, least/list, bead/bid, ease/is, beat/bit

Test   See Overview, pages 7–8. *Answers:*
1. sheep   2. hills   3. chicks   4. fill   5. leave.

Practice 2   See Overview, page 8.
  Other words from the dialogue with the sound ɪ: in, it, if, sick, miss, Billy, begins, six, coming. (The words *here* and the unstressed *we'll* may also have the sound ɪ.)
Note:

1. Some students find the pronunciation of *it's* difficult; occasionally what is taken to be a mistake in grammar (**Is a book*) may in part be a pronunciation problem. Check students' pronunciation of *it's*. If they have difficulty pronouncing the word, practice forward and backward buildup with the aid of the blackboard:
  it   it's
  s   ts   it's

2. Some students pronounce *interesting* as "in-te**res**ting" (four syllables, with main stress on the third syllable). Native English speakers generally say ɪntrəstɪŋ (three syllables, with stress on the first syllable). Use the blackboard to show a simplified transcription of the word: "INtresting." If students have difficulty, have them compare their pronunciation with yours or with the pronunciation on the Cassette. How many syllables

does the word have? Which syllable has the stress?

Dialogue   See Overview, pages 8–9. *Note:* Billy the Kid was a nineteenth-century American outlaw. Many stories have been told and several movies have been made about him.

Stress   Students often confuse numbers like *fourteen* fɔrtiyn and *forty* fɔrtiy. Particularly when there is some question about which number was said, they may stress the last syllable of *forty*, in an attempt to be clear, making the problem worse. Note that when counting – thirteen, fourteen, fifteen, and so on – people tend to stress the first syllable of each word more than they would when using the word in other contexts. Since students usually learn numbers by counting, they then have difficulty in stressing these words correctly so as to distinguish them from thirty, forty, fifty, and so forth. (When thirteen, fourteen, fifteen, etc., are used before a noun, they also tend to be stressed on the first syllable – **thir**teen **books, four**teen **stu**dents – making the situation even more confusing.) Students may find it helpful to know that numbers such as thirteen, fourteen, and fifteen are stressed on the first syllable only in special situations: (1) when counting; (2) when they come before some nouns; and (3) when two are contrasted: "I said **thir**teen, not **six**teen." Otherwise, the final syllables of the words should be stressed. Also note that in American English, the pronunciation of t in *-teen/-ty* varies along with the stress. At the beginning of stressed *-teen*, t is voiceless and aspirated (pronounced with a puff of air). In unstressed *-ty* (except in *fifty* and *sixty*), it is pronounced more like a quick English d. (See Unit 23.)

Steps:

1. Students read or repeat the numbers, reading the columns horizontally. Emphasize stress by, say, tapping with a ruler.

2. Write the numbers from the last two columns on the blackboard. Ask a student to stand at the blackboard and point to the numbers as you say them. Then other students should take turns

saying the numbers clearly enough for a student to point to the correct ones.

Game   Students play in a group of about five people. The person who calls out the numbers should check them off as they are called, without letting the other students see them. Alternatively, write the numbers on small slips of paper that the student can pick up at random.

Spelling   The tendency of many students to confuse the sounds iy and ɪ may be reinforced by confusion over spelling. In many other languages, the letter *i* represents a tense vowel sound resembling English iy. In English, however, the letter *i* usually represents the sound ɪ or ay (see Unit 15), not iy. Although *i* does represent the sound iy in a few words (e.g., *ski* and *police*), it is not a regular spelling for this sound.

Note:

1. Doubling consonants maintains the ɪ sound in words like *bigger* or *beginning*, since the letter *i* followed by a single consonant and then a vowel would normally have the sound ay.

2. *give, live* (verb): English words do not end with the letter *v*. An *e* is always added in the spelling, even if the vowel in the word is "short" (short vowels: ɪ, ɛ, æ, ɑ spelled with the letter *o*, ʌ).

3. *y:* Some people pronounce a final unstressed *y* or *ey* (as in *city, happy, money*) as ɪ. See Unit 1, under Variation.

4. *been:* The word *been* is sometimes pronounced with the vowel ɛ in American English or with the vowel iy in British English.

Note that the spelling list in the Student's Book does not include spellings that represent an unstressed ɪ sound, like the *e* in *example* ɪgzæmpl or in *because*.

Further practice

Have students practice short sentences that contrast the sounds iy and ɪ. For example:

This isn't easy.	Feel this.
Sit in this seat.	Be still!
Did you eat it?	Do you need this?
Did you see it?	Six, please.

Linking pronunciation with other course work

Tie pronunciation in with practice of:

1. it/is/it's/isn't. For example, play the game "20 Questions." In this game, one person thinks of an object (which you can limit in some way, e.g., to items in the classroom), and the others then ask questions to try to identify the object. These questions must be yes/no questions. For example:

Is it bigger than this book? (Yes, it is./No, it isn't.)
Is it alive? (Yes, it is./No, it isn't.)

2. Conditional sentences with *if* (If you're sick, stay home.)

3. *This* vs. *these*

UNIT 3 ε (yes)

Sound production

See Overview, page 5.

Variation   In some (e.g., Southern) dialects of American English, ε may be pronounced like ɪ before a nasal sound such as n so that, for example, *pen* and *pin* may both be pronounced more like pɪn.

Length: See note in Unit 2, under Variation. Compare: *bed/bet, said/set, led/let, peg/peck, edge/etch.*

Student difficulties   Many students do not have difficulty with the sound ε. Some students, however, including speakers of Arabic and some speakers of Dutch, may confuse ε with ɪ. Other students may pronounce ε as too open, causing confusion with æ (e.g., pronouncing *pen* as *pan*). Chinese speakers may confuse ε with ʌ. Some students, including speakers of Spanish and Italian, may pronounce it as a tense rather than a relaxed sound, creating confusion with ey (often substituting a pure tense vowel e for both ε and ey). This problem may be reinforced by spelling,

since in many languages the letter *e* represents the tense vowel e.

Students who pronounce ε either as too closed (ɪ) or too open (æ) may be helped by using a pencil or finger to judge how wide open their mouths should be. Usually, a pencil or finger should just barely fit between the teeth when saying ε. (For ɪ, a fingernail might fit, but not a pencil. For æ, a pencil would fit easily.)

Suggested procedures

Practice 1   See Overview, pages 6–7.

Contrasts for further practice: bitter/better, pick/peck, Ginny/Jenny, if/F, bit/bet, pit/pet, miss/mess, six/sex, lift/left, big/beg, spill/spell, did/dead, wrist/rest, disk/desk

Test   See Overview, pages 7–8. *Answers:*
1. pen   2. bill   3. better   4. Jenny   5. chicks.

Practice 2   See Overview, page 8.

Other words from the dialogue with the sound ε: Ed, cigarette, went, well, yes, very, spent.

Check the pronunciation of *everybody* and *everything*. The second *e* in *every* (and in compounds formed with *every*) is silent: εvriy. If students pronounce the *e*, respell the words on the blackboard as "evrybody, evrything." (The main stress in each word is on the first syllable.)

Dialogue   See Overview, pages 8–9.

After students listen to the dialogue, you may want to ask a few questions that elicit answers using the sound ε. For example:
Who went to Venice?
Did he go by himself?
Why is everyone jealous?
How much money does Ed have left?

Intonation   Some students have difficulty with falling intonation for "wh-questions." It may be helpful to practice with shorter wh-questions before continuing with the lesson. Write the wh-words ("Who?" "What?" etc.) on the blackboard;

students practice saying these with falling intonation. Then practice the questions "What's this/
that?" "Who's this/that?" Point to an object or a
person (pictures can be used), and have students
ask the appropriate question. Demonstrate this
first. Add more questions, using the wh-words
written on the blackboard and objects, pictures,
or written cues as prompts (for example: "What's
her name?" "Where are you from?" "Where do
you live?"). Note that the wh-word is stressed
but said with a level tone; make sure students do
not put a change in intonation (e.g., a rising
tone) here or on the unstressed words.

Note: The actual intonation used by native English speakers may differ from the intonation
shown in the Student's Book (e.g., yes/no questions may not always have a rising tone; statements and wh-questions do not always have a
falling tone). The patterns shown are *general* intonation patterns for each type of sentence – the
intonation most likely to be used with a neutral,
matter-of-fact meaning.

Conversation   Students can practice the conversation either in small groups or as a whole
class. Model the conversation by asking a student the questions. That student then chooses
another student to question, and so on. Other
place names familiar to students that contain the
sound ε can be added.

Note the stress in "How did you spend your
vacation?" The first time it is said as, "**How** did
you **spend** your va**ca**tion?" After that, *your* will
have a contrastive stress: "**How** did you **spend**
your va**ca**tion?"

Spelling   Compare common spelling patterns
for the sounds ε and iy using the letter *e*. Note,
for example, the doubling of the consonant to
maintain the "short" sound ε in words like *getting* and *redder*.

For review, give students a list of words such
as the following. They should indicate whether
the *e* spelling in each word has the sound ε
(Sound 1) or iy (Sound 2).

1. friend   4. _e_verybody
2. complete   5. met
3. piece   6. equal

7. jealous   9. cream
8. meat   10. breakfast

Further practice

The following letters are pronounced with the
sound ε: *f, s, x, l, m,* and *n*. If students have
trouble with oral spelling, have them say these
letters aloud. Then write a few words using
these letters (such as the ones below) on the
blackboard, and ask them to spell the words
aloud.

left   excellent
many   lesson
Mexican   listen
lemon   spelling

Linking pronunciation with other course work

Tie pronunciation in with practice of:

1. Comparatives with *better*. For example, write
on the blackboard, "Ellen, Fred, Ed, and Jenny
all did well on a test."

Ellen Fred Ed   Jenny
90%   93%   96% 98%

Point first to *Jenny*, then to *Ellen*. As you point,
ask: "Did Jenny do better than Ellen?" (Answer:
"Yes.") Then point first to *Ellen*, then *Ed*: "Did
Ellen do better than Ed?" (Answer: "No. Ed did
better than Ellen.") Write the model questions
and answers on the blackboard, if necessary.
Then, as you point to names, students ask and
answer questions following the model. For
example:

Jenny . . . Fred   Ed . . . Fred
Ellen . . . Fred   Ellen . . . Jenny
Ed . . . Jenny   etc.

2. Wh-questions

3. Talking about vacations: "How did you spend
your vacation?" "I went to . . ."

4. Offering food at a social function: "Have some

bread/a cookie." "Help yourself to coffee/cake/ cookies."

Word stress practice

1. everything   everyone   everybody   everywhere
   anything   anyone   anybody   anywhere
   something   someone   somebody   somewhere
   nothing   no one   nobody   nowhere

Write some of these words on the blackboard or on flash cards. Say a few of the words, and have the students repeat them. Tap out the stress if necessary, or show a large dot over the stressed syllable and smaller dots over the other syllables. Then point to other words (or add them to the list); have students try pronouncing them. Note that all these compounds have a strong stress on the first syllable.

2. Practice stress on reflexive pronouns, following the same procedure:
   yourself   myself
   ourselves   herself
   himself   themselves

Here, the stress is on the second syllable.

UNIT 4 ey (train) *eeei*

Sound production

See Overview, page 5.
   Note: Students should make their muscles tense for the sound **ey**.

Variation   Length: See note in Unit 1 (under Variation). Compare *plays/place, stayed/state, played/plate, age/H.*
   Note: In British English, this sound is always a diphthong.

Student difficulties   Many students do not have trouble producing a sound close to **ey**. In many languages, however, there is only one vowel sound in the area of **ey** and **ɛ** – a pure tense vowel **e**. Speakers of these languages are likely to substitute this **e** sound for **ey** in English

oso

and/or to confuse **ey** and **ɛ**. They may also make the sound too short. Students who tend to have difficulty with **ey** include speakers of Arabic, French, Italian, Greek, Hebrew, Japanese, Korean, Thai, German, Russian, and Scandinavian languages. Although the most common error is to confuse **ey** with **ɛ**, some students may confuse **ey** with **ay**, and others (e.g., Scandinavian and sometimes Spanish speakers) may make the second part of the diphthong too long. Some students (such as Chinese speakers) may find this sound difficult to say before a final consonant and may tend to drop that consonant.

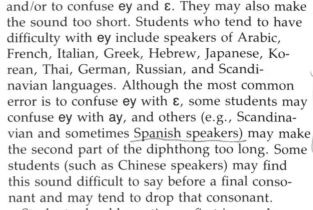

   Students should practice **ey** first in words where it is most easily distinguished from **ɛ** – in words where it is longest and has a strong **y** glide sound (at the end of a word, as in *say,* or before a voiced consonant, as in *days* or *train*). (In an unstressed syllable, there may be no glide at all.) Emphasizing the gradual change in lip position in saying **ey** may also help students.

Suggested procedures

Practice 1   See Overview, pages 6–7.
   Contrasts for further practice relevant to student difficulties:
ɛ/ey   fell/fail, sell/sail, shed/shade, letter/later, edge/age, Ed/aid, chess/chase, get/gate, let/late, west/waist, men/main
ay/ey   I/A, my/may, why/way, like/lake, die/day, bike/bake

Test   See Overview, pages 7–8. *Answers:*
1. pepper   2. pen   3. sail   4. taste   5. shed.

Practice 2   See Overview, page 8.
   Other words from the dialogue with the sound **ey**: day, May, take, vacation.

Dialogue   See Overview, pages 8–9.
   Call attention to the pronunciation of *say* and *says* (both used in the dialogue). Pronounce the two words (*say* **sey**; *says* **sɛz**). After the students

ey — e — ɛ

listen to the pronunciations, ask them if the vowel was the same in both words.

Intonation Students here practice intonation in questions expressing surprise. In these questions, the person repeats something that the first speaker said, but with rising intonation to indicate surprise or skepticism. The greater the surprise felt, the more the intonation is likely to rise. (In any case, the rise here is likely to be higher than the rise for an ordinary yes/no question.) If students do not use the right intonation – for example, if their intonation sounds too flat – use hand gestures or arrows drawn on the blackboard to contrast their intonation with the intonation they should be using.

Extension If students have difficulty (for example, in using a wide enough range of intonation), give them additional practice. Make surprising or untrue statements, and have them repeat the part of the sentence that is surprising, using the appropriate intonation. For example:
TEACHER: Tomorrow is Sunday. (or whatever
           day it is not)
STUDENTS: Sunday?

   Today's class will last for six hours.
   Paris is the largest city in the world.
   I was born in 1855.
   I'm going to give you a test now.

Conversation Students practice the conversation, following the example. After completing the conversation, they should switch roles and repeat it.

Spelling See Unit 5 to compare common spelling patterns for the sounds **ey** and **æ** using the letter *a*.

Note:

1. The spelling *ea* has the sound **ey** in only a few words (it usually has the sound **iy**). Students should memorize these words.

2. The word *gray* is also spelled *grey* (especially in British English).

Further practice

1. Write the following limerick on the blackboard. Have students fill in the incomplete lines and read the poem aloud:
   A gray old lady from Spain
   Was afraid to fly on a . . .
   But she went up one day
   And she said, "It's O . . ."
   It's better than going by . . .
   [Answers: plane, K, train]

2. Spelling: Letters of the alphabet with the sound **ey**: *a, h, j,* and *k*.

Linking pronunciation with other course work

Tie pronunciation in with practice in:

1. Saying dates. For example:
   What's today's date?
   the eighth of May/May eighth
   the eighteenth of April/April eighteenth
   the twenty-eighth of May/May twenty-eighth
   (or just "the eighth," "the eighteenth," etc.)

2. Polite apologies beginning with "I'm afraid . . ." For example:
   I'm afraid you've made a mistake/you'll have
      to wait/you're too late.
   I'm afraid I've forgotten your name/I'm late/I
      broke the plate/I've lost your paper/I don't
      have any change.
Briefly describe for students situations that would call for apologies like these; students supply appropriate apologies.

Word stress practice

See Overview, pages 11–12.
Recognition test: A ● •   B • ●
1. today [B]   4. afraid [B]
2. mistake [B]   5. railroad [A]
3. April [A]   6. station [A]

7. surprise [B]   9. away [B]
8. birthday [A]   10. repeat [B]

UNIT 5 æ (hat)

Sound production

See Overview, page 5.

Variation   Length: See note in Unit 2 (under Variation). Compare: *bag/back, cab/cap, sad/sat, have* (or *halve*)/*half.*

Many speakers use a slightly different pronunciation of æ in some or all words, with the tongue higher and the lips less open. Some add a short ə glide, especially when æ is said by itself or before a voiced consonant (as in *hand* or *bad*). In some words where most American and Canadian speakers use æ, British speakers say ɑ (for example, in *dance, glass,* and *laugh*).

Student difficulties   Almost all students have difficulty with the sound æ. Speakers of Dutch, German, Turkish, Farsi, Russian, Scandinavian, and Indian languages usually confuse it with ɛ, resulting in confusion between words like *pan* and *pen*. French, Italian, Spanish, Portuguese, Greek, Japanese, Swahili, and West African speakers confuse it with ʌ (as in *hut*) and/or ɑ (as in *hot*). French, Italian, Greek, and Swahili speakers may also confuse it with ɛ. Chinese students often nasalize æ; they also may confuse it with the sounds ɛ, ʌ, or ɑ. Thai students often pronounce it as too long. Many languages do not have the English sounds æ or ɑ but do have a sound that is somewhere between the two English sounds; students often substitute this sound for æ in English. This non-English sound is usually spelled with the letter *a* in these languages, increasing students' confusion.

It may be helpful for students who have difficulty with æ to spend some time on the mouth position. The mouth should be open enough so that a finger or pencil can fit easily between the teeth. The tongue should rest at the bottom of the mouth with the tip placed against the bottom

teeth. Students should move the tongue down a little from its position for ɛ, but they should not move it back.

Suggested procedures

Practice 1   See Overview, pages 6–7.
Contrasts for further practice: left/laughed, send/sand, dead/Dad, set/sat, met/mat, bet/bat, pet/pat, M/am, bed/bad, head/had, Ed/add, end/and, guess/gas, ten/tan, bend/band, lend/land, dense/dance, Beth/bath, peck/pack, shell/shall, gem/jam, better/batter, letter/latter

Test   See Overview, pages 7–8. *Answers:*
1. men   2. pan   3. laughed   4. sad   5. dead.

Practice 2   See Overview, page 8.
Other words from the dialogue with the sound æ: had, ran, after, that, fast, last, back, thank you.
Note: The words *and* and *at* usually contain the sound ə in connected speech. The words *have* and *can* at the beginning of a question can have either the sound ə or æ.

Dialogue   See Overview, pages 8–9.
Note: Make sure students do not add an extra syllable for the *-ed* in *grabbed, happened, robbed, stuffed* (see Unit 24). If students have difficulty pronouncing these words, write them on the blackboard, drawing a line through the *e*, or re-spell them (as, for example, "grabd" and "happend").

Sentence stress   In this section of the Student's Book normal sentence stress is practiced, with the main stress on the last important word in the sentence. The second and third sentences practice normal adjective/modifier + noun stress. Both adjective and noun are stressed, with greater stress on the noun.

Students listen to and repeat the sentences on the Cassette. Note that all of the sentences have four major stresses but that the rhythm of each sentence is different. Tap with a ruler or clap to show the rhythm. For the first sentence, show the rhythm and how the unstressed words are quieter and shorter than the stressed words by saying it using nonsense syllables: DAH də DAH dədə DAH də DAH. For the second and third sentences it may be helpful to use backward and forward buildup to practice the stress:

black pants
the black pants
with the black pants
the man with the black pants
Do you mean
Do you mean the man with the black pants?

Conversation   Students practice the conversation, following the example. Practice the words below the pictures first, checking the stress for adjective + noun, with the main stress on the noun. (Changing the stress would change the meaning. When the main stress is put on the adjective, it generally means that two adjectives are being contrasted: "Do you mean the man with the black **pants**?" "No. The man with the **blue** pants.")

Spelling   Compare common spelling patterns for the sounds æ and ey using the letter *a*. Note the doubling of the consonant to maintain the æ sound in words like *sadder, fatter, fattest, grabbed,* and *grabbing*. Note that at the end of English words like *have* an *e* is added after the *v*, even if the vowel is short, like æ.

   Give students a written list of words (suggestions are given below). Students say whether the *a* spelling in each word has the sound æ or ey.

1. ages
2. mistake
3. family
4. change
5. jacket
6. grabbed
7. famous
8. happen
9. waiting
10. April

Linking pronunciation with other course work

Tie pronunciation in with practice of:

1. Short answers with *am, can/can't, have/haven't, has/hasn't*: Yes, I am./Yes, she can./No, they

haven't./etc. If necessary, first practice from the blackboard:

Yes,	I	am.		No,	I	can't.
		can.				haven't.
		have.				hasn't.
	he	has.			he	
	she				she	

Then have students give short answers to rapid oral questions. Choose questions at random from those below, or make questions relevant to particular students.

a. Are you | studying English | ?
	listening
	(student's name)
	(student's nationality)
	hungry

b. Can you | understand (student's or another language) | ?
	speak (student's or another language)
	drive a car
	dance
	play the guitar

c. Have you ever | been to Japan | ?
| | been to France |

2. Describing people to show which one is meant. For example:
   Look at that man.
   Which one? The man with the black pants?
   No. That one with the camera.

Word stress practice

1. Matching exercise: Read the words in Column A aloud. For each word, students find a word in Column B that has the same stress pattern (students can draw a line connecting the two words or say the answers aloud).

A	B
1. plastic	absolutely
2. understand	again
3. detective	afternoon
4. suddenly	exactly
5. police	jacket
6. conversation	manager

Answers: 1. plastic/jacket   2. understand/ afternoon   3. detective/exactly   4. suddenly/ manager   5. police/again   6. conversation/ absolutely.

2. Adding suffixes: Most English suffixes are not stressed. Although some cause a change in stress when they are added to a word (e.g., photo-graph – photography), many suffixes do not. Have students practice adding suffixes like *-er*, *-ly*, and *-ing*, which cause no change in stress:

   rob – robber; manage – manager
   exact – exactly; sudden – suddenly; usual – usually
   run – running; wear – wearing; work – working

UNIT 6 Review

This unit provides additional practice and review of the vowels iy, ɪ, ɛ, ey, and æ, taught in Units 1 through 5. *Note:* The set of words with con-trasting vowels at the beginning of the Review is not on the Cassette. Before proceeding, you may want to have students listen to and repeat some or all of these words, reading across, or reading first down and then across.

Listening practice

Students write down or say aloud the number of the vowel they hear in each word as it is said by the teacher or on the Cassette. *Answers:* led; beat; lid; Dane; seal; bat; den; bit; lead; Dan.

Pronunciation practice

See Overview, page 8.
   Other words from the dialogue with the vowel sounds practiced in Units 1 through 5: we, is, this, in, yes, let's, Ben, any, cake, having, shall, Ann.
   Note: When unstressed, the word *and* usually

has the vowel sound ə or no vowel at all. When unstressed, the word *any* may also have the sound ə.

Dialogue

See Overview, pages 8–9.
   Say each line from the dialogue; students re-peat chorally. While saying each sentence, tap or clap to show its rhythm and stress pattern, if necessary. Then have students practice the dia-logue in pairs.

Jumbled spellings

Students unscramble the jumbled spellings to form words. Have them read their answers aloud, with one student writing the answers on the blackboard. Ask which vowel sound each word has (use the numbers from the Listening Practice at the beginning of the unit). You may also want to have students spell the words aloud to review oral spellings (note that most of the let-ters also use the vowels being reviewed).
   Answers: 1. hand (Sound 5)   2. lip (Sound 2)   3. teeth (Sound 1)   4. face (Sound 3)   5. chest (Sound 4)   If you have a problem with your teeth, you see a *dentist.*

Spelling review

Give students a list of words, on paper or on the blackboard, which have the sounds practiced in Units 1 through 5. Students sort the words by sound, grouping words with the same vowel sound together. Alternatively, prepare a group activity by writing each word on a card or a small piece of paper (prepare more than one set of cards for larger classes). Working in groups, students read the words aloud and group to-gether the ones that have the same sound.

Sample list of words to be given in scrambled order:

iy please, people, thirteen, these, leave
ɪ minute, women, quick, English, miss
ɛ says, friend, jealous, shelf, any
ey steak, they, wait, late, change, eight
æ black, laugh, happen, glasses, cash

Word stress recognition test

See Overview, pages 11–12.

A ● · B · ●

1. review [B]   6. complete [B]
2. salad [A]   7. lemon [A]
3. minutes [A]   8. begin [B]
4. jacket [A]   9. happen [A]
5. yourself [B]   10. mistake [B]

UNIT 7 ʌ (cup)

Sound production

See Overview, page 5.

Variation   Length: See the note in Unit 2.
Compare: *buzz/bus, cub/cup, dug/duck, bud/but*.

Student difficulties   Most students have difficulty with the sound ʌ. Many substitute ɑ or a sound from their own language that is between English ɑ and æ, often creating confusion in English between both ʌ and æ (as in *cut/cat*) and ʌ and ɑ (as in *cut/cot*). Students likely to replace ʌ with æ, ɑ, or a similar sound include speakers of Italian, Japanese, Spanish, Greek, Portuguese, Arabic, Farsi, Chinese, and African languages. French speakers may substitute a sound similar to ɜ (without a following r). Some students may pronounce ʌ too far back in the mouth, creating confusion with ɔ or ʊ. Many students, even those who can pronounce ʌ, have problems with ʌ that are caused by spelling. They may pronounce the letter *o* as ow or ɑ in words where it represents the sound ʌ, saying, for example, lowv for *love* or nɑθɪŋ for *nothing*. Or, they may

use the sound uw in words where ʌ is spelled with the letter *u*, as in *study* or *bus*.

If students substitute ɑ for ʌ, tell them to close their mouths a little and move their tongues just a little further forward. If they make a sound like æ, tell them to relax their mouths, especially their lips, which should be pulled back a little for æ, but not for ʌ.

Suggested procedures

Practice 1   See Overview, pages 6–7.
Contrasts for further practice relevant to student difficulties:

æ/ʌ cat/cut, bat/but, fan/fun, match/much, cab/cub, track/truck, ankle/uncle, mad/mud, calf/cuff, tan/ton, dam/dumb, bad/bud, lack/luck, lamp/lump, sadden/sudden, rang/rung, sang/sung, drank/drunk, sank/sunk, swam/swum
ʊ/ʌ See Teacher's Manual, Unit 12.

Test   See Overview, pages 7–8. *Answers:*
1. bug   2. cup   3. rag   4. ran   5. uncle.

Practice 2   See Overview, page 8.

Dialogue   See Overview, pages 8–9.
Note: Although many words spelled with the letter *o* in the dialogue have the sound ʌ, not all words with this spelling have this sound. Check to make sure students realize that *don't* and *so* have a different sound (ow, Unit 11).

Intonation   Students practice intonation used for items in a list. Each item is usually pronounced with rising intonation, except for the last item, which has falling intonation.

Game   Each student repeats what preceding students said and then adds a new item to the list, as in the example. The game ends when the list becomes too long for students to remember it. Students should practice the list of items first; explain any new vocabulary. Check stress, making sure students do not stress the words *a*, *of*, or *some*.

For more advanced students To make the activity more challenging, students can play the game with their books closed after practicing the words in the list.

Spelling Problems with the sound ʌ are often complicated by confusions caused by spelling. All of the spellings for this sound are also used as spellings for other sounds – often for sounds that may themselves be confused with the sound ʌ by students.

The letter *u* is a common spelling for the sounds ʊ and uw, as well as for ʌ. Note the doubling of the consonant to keep the short ʌ sound (rather than uw) in words such as *sunny* and *cutting*.

The letter *o* usually has the sound ow or ɑ. Before the consonants *n, m, v,* and voiced *th,* it often has the sound ʌ.

Note:

ou (*country, touch,* etc.): usually has the sound ɑw.

oo (*blood, flood*): usually has the sound ʊ or uw.

oe (*does, doesn't*): usually has the sound ow.

As a review activity at another time, ask students for words spelled with the letter *o* and pronounced with the sound ʌ; write them on the blackboard.

Linking pronunciation with other course work

Tie pronunciation in with practice of:

1. Family relationships. Draw a family tree on the blackboard.

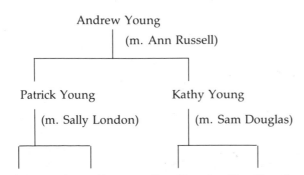

Students practice the pronunciation of the following words from the blackboard or flash cards: mother, son, husband, brother, uncle, cousin, grandmother, grandson, mother-in-law, and brother-in-law. Practice the names; if necessary, check that students know which are boys' names and which are girls' names.

As you point to names on the family tree, have students make sentences that describe the relationships.

Examples:

(point to) Kathy Young, Pam Douglas
(say) "Kathy Young is Pam Douglas's mother."
(point to) Sam Douglas, Kathy Young
(say) "Sam Douglas is Kathy Young's husband."

Note that each sentence will have five strong stresses; the sentences should all take about the same amount of time to say. Tap the strong stresses with a ruler to demonstrate speed and rhythm. Tap again as students say one of the sentences.

2. Short answers using *does/doesn't*

3. Questions with *How much*

4. *Must*

5. Past participles (contrasted with other forms of the verb):

ring/rang/rung, sing/sang/sung, drink/drank/ drunk, sink/sank/sunk, stink/stank/stunk, shrink/shrank/shrunk, swim/swam/swum, begin/began/begun

run/ran/run, hang/hung/hung, swing/swung/ swung, come/came/come, become/became/ become, come/came/come, cut/cut/cut, shut/ shut/shut, stick/stuck/stuck, sting/stung/ stung, win/won/won, do/did/done

Write past participles, selected from the list above, on slips of paper, and put the slips in a bag or box. Divide the class into two teams. A student from team A picks a slip and reads the participle aloud. A person from team B then supplies the past tense form. If the past tense is correct, team B gets a point, and someone else on team B says the present (infinitive) form of the verb (team B gets another point if this is correct). If the past or present form is wrong, the turn passes to team A. For the next verb, someone from team B selects the slip, and so on.

Word stress practice

Read the following pairs of words. Students indicate whether the stress pattern for each pair was the same or different.

1. nothing, funny [S]
2. company, unhappy [D]
3. understand, government [D]
4. remember, unhappy [S]
5. comfortable, wonderful [S]
6. butterfly, umbrella [D]
7. sunglasses, grandmother [S]
8. unusual, uninteresting [S]

Either before or after doing this, students should listen to and repeat the words. Tap or clap to show the stress pattern. Point out that in words with the prefix *un*, the *un* generally does not have the main stress. If possible, ask for or provide other words with the prefix *un* that students know (such as *uncomfortable*).

UNIT 8 Part 1
ə (a banana)

Note: This unit is divided into two parts. For lower level classes it might be best to teach these on separate days.

Some people use the symbol ə to represent the stressed vowels ʌ and ɜr. In this book the symbol ə is reserved for unstressed vowels only. In the units on ə in the Student's Book, a dot is shown under vowels pronounced as ə, since the normal spellings do not help to make students aware of this sound.

Sound production

See Overview, page 5.

Note:

1. The tongue should rest relaxed in the middle of the mouth, as for the sound ʌ. The lips should be in a neutral position (not rounded), with the mouth almost closed (not opened wide, as for ɑ).

2. If the sound ə is said in isolation, it is automatically stressed. The sound will then no longer be ə, but ʌ (or another vowel).

Variation   The vowel in many reduced syllables may vary between ə and ɪ. Some people may pronounce the unstressed vowel in some of the words in this unit, for example, with an unstressed ɪ sound.

Student difficulties   The sound ə (the schwa) is the most frequently used vowel sound in English. Almost all students have some difficulty with it, even though it may not be a difficult sound for them to pronounce. Students commonly substitute a sound suggested by the spelling that ə has in a word.

Many languages do not have the sound ə and, in fact, may not have reduced vowels at all. In English, unstressed syllables are shorter than stressed syllables and tend to be pronounced with an unclear, reduced, neutral-sounding vowel, usually ə (or ɪ). In many other languages, such as Spanish, French, Italian, Greek, Brazilian Portuguese, Farsi, Thai, West African languages, and Swahili, syllables that are not stressed may take as long to say as stressed syllables and may be pronounced with full, clear vowels. Even speakers of languages that have a reduced vowel like ə may have difficulty with ə in English. In other languages, the sound may not be as reduced or may not occur as frequently as it does in English, and it may always be spelled with the same letter (e.g., the letter *e* in Scandinavian languages and in German).

Students have particular difficulty with words that have "weak forms" – words like *and, as, have, do, to,* and *from* that may be pronounced with a full vowel when they are said alone but that tend to be unstressed and pronounced with the sound ə in connected speech. Note that when these words are said in isolation, they are automatically stressed. Students usually learn these words in isolation and tend to carry over this strong, stressed pronunciation into their speech. This tendency is reinforced by what they see in the spelling of the words. Students also often have difficulty hearing these weak forms when said by native speakers and may perceive English speakers as "swallowing their words." Trying to reduce the stress on weak forms or on unstressed syllables can prove so difficult for students that they will just drop the unstressed word or syllable.

Students at an intermediate or advanced level often continue to have difficulty with ə. The reasons for this may include (1) that they simply were not taught to use ə from the beginning of their language studies or that they did not use it with such great frequency as the sound actually occurs in English, finding it difficult to change habits later on; (2) that there is no indication in spelling to show where ə should be used; (3) that students can get away without using it (although they may not always understand native speakers, they themselves will probably be understood); and (4) a mistaken idea that the use of the schwa is sloppy or careless and that speech is more correct or more easily understood if the speaker uses full vowels.

Since schwa occurs so frequently and is such an alien concept for many students, it is important to teach it at an early stage, so that students get accustomed to using it and hearing it.

Suggested procedures

Practice 1   Students look at and repeat the words in their books. Call their attention to the places where ə is shown by a dot. Point out that different letters spell the sound ə: here, *a, e, i,* and *o.*

Demonstrate the stress patterns of the words by, say, tapping with a ruler. Then have students tap while repeating the words again. Point out that ə is never in the stressed part of a word or sentence. Discuss the use of ə in the weak forms of *a, an,* and *some:* ə, ən, səm. If students

have difficulty, respell *some* on the blackboard: "s'm."

Note: In English, *chocolate* is usually pronounced with two syllables, with stress on the first: tʃɔklət. Students may substitute a pronunciation from their own language, often pronouncing both the second *o* and final *e,* with stress on the third syllable. An "international" word like this can be useful in demonstrating differences in stress and pronunciation patterns between languages.

Practice 2   Students practice the weak form of *of:* əv (in relaxed speech, often reduced to just ə, especially before a consonant). Students look at the picture and repeat the phrase for the first item in each pair, and then make a parallel phrase, substituting the word for the second item. Make sure students do not stress weak forms or other unstressed syllables. Tap to show stress, or write phrases on the blackboard, showing stressed syllables and ə (for example: ə CUP ə COFfee).

Practice 3   Pronunciation of *can:* weak form (in the middle of a sentence) – kən; in yes/no questions – kæn or weak form kən; in the affirmative short answer – kæn. (*Note:* Make sure students do not confuse the auxiliary verb *can* with the noun *can* [kæn] used in Practice 2.) The word *can't* is always stressed and pronounced with a full vowel: kænt. Some speakers make a distinction between the vowels in *can't* and in the strong form of *can* (e.g., pronouncing *can* with a vowel like ɛ).

Pronunciation of *the:* weak form before a consonant – ðə.

Students look at the pictures and repeat the sentences, first reading down the columns and then across. Tap to show stress; each affirmative statement has two strong stresses. Respell the weak form on the blackboard, if necessary: "kən" (or "c'n"). Discuss the pronunciation rules given above. Note that in the middle of a sentence, often the only noticeable difference in sound between *can* and *can't* is in the sound of the vowel: ə versus æ. The substitution of a full vowel for ə in *can* may lead to frequent misunderstandings, with the opposite meaning understood from what was intended.

After students practice affirmative and negative statements, have them practice questions and short answers, first replying to questions asked by the teacher ("Can she swim?," etc.) and then asking and answering questions among themselves.

Test See Overview, pages 7–8. *Answers:*
1. can't   2. can   3. can   4. can, can't   5. can't.

UNIT 8 Part 2 ər (letter)

Sound production

See Overview, page 5.
Note: The sound ər is the same as ɜr, but unstressed. As with plain ə, ər does not occur when stressed or said in isolation.

Practice 4 Students listen to and repeat words ending with the sound ər. (Note the different spellings for this sound in *painter, actor,* and *picture.*) Students tend to have the same difficulties with ər as they do with ə alone, replacing it with a vowel suggested by the written form and usually adding a non-English (e.g., trilled or flapped) r sound. To discourage students from stressing the sound ər here or pronouncing it with a distinct vowel, respell words on the blackboard, omitting the vowel ("paintr," "doctr," etc.).

Students practice questions and answers about the pictures, as in the example. Note the weak form of *does:* dəz.
Note: Stronger stress on the first word in *cab driver, bank teller,* and *police officer;* stress on both words in *computer programmer.*

Dialogue See Overview, pages 8–9.
Where more than one possible word or phrase is given to complete a sentence, only the first one is said on the Cassette. The other word or phrase can be used for additional practice later by the students.

Words that have weak forms pronounced with the sound ə: *a, an, the, some, of, from, at, to, for, can, do, you, and, but, that.*

Note:

1. Weak form of *and:* ən or n (the d is usually dropped).

2. *that:* Students may be confused by the different uses and pronunciations of *that.* In "Not that supermarket" or "Oh, that one," *that* is a demonstrative, contrasting with *this.* It is stressed and pronounced with a full vowel: ðæt. When *that* is used as a connecting word (e.g., "the one that's near . . .") it is usually unstressed; in rapid speech native speakers would tend to say ðət.

3. Strong stress on the first element in *supermarket, drugstore, movie theater, record store, tuna fish,* and *address book.*

Spelling The great variety of spellings for the sound ə naturally add to its difficulty for students.
Many common beginnings and endings for words with these various spellings usually have the sound ə. For example:
a- (about, across, around)
-al, -ant, -ance, -acy, -ace, -man, -graphy, -able/-ible (musical, industrial, pleasant, assistant, assistance, democracy, surface, policeman, woman, biography, available, possible)
-el, -en, -ence, -ent, -ment (marvel, happen, kitchen, independence, excellent, president, apartment)
com-, con-, pro-, to- (compare, continue, protect, today)
-ion, -some, -ogy, -ophy (question, opinion, handsome, biology, philosophy)
-ous (famous, nervous, delicious)
-er, -ar, -or, -ure (painter, sugar, actor, picture)
Note, too, some common words that can have the sound ə in a sentence (weak forms):
a, an, am, and, as, at
for, from, of, to
the

Review Write the words below on the blackboard or on a paper handout. For each word, have students put a dot under the letter(s) with the sound ə. (This may be done with or without reading the words aloud.)

1. about	6. apartment
2. today	7. complete
3. telephone	8. breakfast
4. famous	9. polite
5. success	10. problem

Further practice

1. *can/can't*: Students practice asking and answering questions about abilities. For example:

A: Can you ride a bike?
B: Yes, I can./No, I can't.

Students practice in pairs, later reporting to the class.

2. Students read these riddles from the blackboard and try to answer them. Put a dot under the letters pronounced as ə, if necessary.

a. What is it? I cạn see it bụt you can't.
b. What is it? You cạn see it bụt I can't.

(Answers: a. The back of your head.   b. The back of my head.)

Linking pronunciation with other course work

Tie pronunciation in with practice of:

1. *can/can't* in talking about abilities;

2. Requests in a restaurant or store using the weak form of *of*; for example: a glass/bottle of water/juice/wine, etc.; a box/pound of rice/cookies, etc.

3. *can* in requests; for example:

  a. Can I have some water/butter/pepper/salt and pepper/bread and butter, please?

  b. A. Can I have an apple/orange/onion/egg/a cookie/banana/cracker, please?
    B: Yes, of course.
    A: Can I have another apple, please?
    B: Sorry. There aren't any more apples.

4. Talking about occupations.

Word stress practice

See Overview, pages 11–12.
Recognition Test: A ● ● ●   B ● ● ●

1. reporter [B]	6. carpenter [A]
2. together [B]	7. bananas [B]
3. terrible [A]	8. designer [B]
4. apartment [B]	9. syllable [A]
5. excellent [A]	10. officer [A]

UNIT 9 ɑ (father)

Sound production

See Overview, page 5.

Variation   In words spelled with *o* where most North Americans say ɑ (*clock, hot, modern,* etc.), British speakers usually have a different vowel sound – ɒ, a sound somewhere between the vowels ɑ and ɔ.

British speakers use the sound ɑ in some words where most North Americans use the vowel æ (e.g., *class, bath, laugh, dance, fast,* and *can't*).

Student difficulties   Students generally do not have difficulty producing a sound close to English ɑ, although sometimes they make the sound too short where it should be lengthened (as in *father*). This sound is often confused with the sounds æ, ʌ, and ɔ, for which students often substitute ɑ, so that the words *cat, cut,* and *caught* may all be pronounced as *cot*. Problems also arise because of spelling. In words spelled with the letter *o* and pronounced with ɑ (e.g., *not*), students often substitute a sound like ow or ɔ.

Suggested procedures

Practice 1 and 2   See Overview, pages 6–7.
Contrasts for further practice relevant to student difficulties:

æ/ɑ map/mop, pat/pot, tap/top, backs/box, add/odd, bland/blond, ax/ox, black/block, band/bond, ma'am/Mom, lack/lock

ʌ/ɑ color/collar, duck/dock, luck/lock, stuck/stock, nut/not, shut/shot, come/calm, rub/rob, gulf/golf, done/Don, bucks/box, muddle/model, rubber/robber, jug/jog, dull/doll

Test   See Overview, pages 7–8. *Answers:*
1. sock 2. cat 3. cup 4. map 5. color
6. dock.

Practice 3   See Overview, page 8.
Other words from the dialogue that may have the sound ɑ: start, washable, Starwash, everybody, what's, water.

Note:

1. Dialect variation: Many people say the words *water, want, horrible, wash,* and *washable* with the sound ɔ rather than ɑ.

2. The vowel in *everybody* and *what's* is often said as ʌ or ə rather than ɑ.

Dialogue   See Overview, pages 8–9.
Students listen to the "TV commercial" with their books closed. They can later practice the dialogue in groups as a role-play, taking turns performing in front of the class to judge which group presents the commercial most effectively.
Note: Pronunciation of *don't* (downt) and *does* (dʌz): Make sure students do not substitute ɑ in these words.

Intonation   Students listen and repeat, practicing strongly falling intonation in exclamations of surprise. In an exclamation, the voice usually rises to a higher tone on the last stressed syllable than it does in an ordinary statement, followed by a sharp fall.
Many students' intonations may tend to sound flat to native English speakers (though British speakers tend to use a wider voice range than Americans). Factors contributing to this flatness

may include feelings of inhibition, lack of confidence, differences in intonation patterns in students' own languages, or simply lack of attention to intonation because of concern with other elements of speech.
Model the appropriate intonation here. If students do not use a wide enough range of intonation, use hand gestures or draw arrows on the blackboard to show the restricted range used by students and the wider range they should be using.
Note: Stress here is normal adjective + noun stress (main stress on the noun).

Conversation   Students practice exclamations, using adjectives from the list to make sentences about the pictures. Practice the words in the list and under the pictures first.

Spelling   The spelling *o* for the sound ɑ causes confusion; students commonly substitute a sound like ɔ or ow when they see this spelling, pronouncing *not*, for example, like *nought* or *note*. Before a consonant at the end of a word (especially before the sounds b, p, t, d, k, ʃ, tʃ, dʒ, and l) or before a doubled consonant in the middle of a word, the letter *o* usually has the sound ɑ. Examples include *job, stop, not, clock, Scotch, doll, bottle,* and *possible*.
Note the doubling of the consonant to maintain the ɑ sound, rather than the sound ow, in words like *shopping, stopped,* and *hotter*; compare *hopping/hoping*.
The spelling *a* also causes some confusion. Note that the letter *a* commonly has the sound ɑ only in the following places: before *r* (as in *star*); before *lm* (as in *calm*; the *l* is silent here); after *w* or *qu* (as in *watch* or *quality*); at the end of a syllable (as in *ma, uh!*); and in the word *father*.
Review sounds spelled with the letter *a*. Give students a list of words such as the following. Have students look at the words and decide which sound the letter *a* has in each one: Sound 1 æ (hat), Sound 2 ey (train), or Sound 3 ɑ (father).

1. glasses [1]	4. hard [3]
2. bank [1]	5. change [2]
3. station [2]	6. calm [3]

7. cash [1]   9. mistake [2]
8. want [3]   10. happen [1]

Linking pronunciation with other course work

Tie pronunciation in with practice of:

1. "What's the matter?/What's the problem?" "I have a headache/backache/stomachache," etc. Note the use of vowels practiced in previous units.

2. Exclamations expressing surprise. For example: "Look at that/Just look at that/What a/Isn't that a beautiful carpet!"

3. Short answers with *are*: "Yes, we are./No, they aren't." *Note:* Pronunciation of *are*: In yes/no questions – ɑr or weak form ər; in the affirmative short answer – ɑr; pronunciation of *aren't* – ɑrnt or ɑrənt.

Word stress practice

One word in each group has a different stress pattern than the other words. Students say which word is different.

	1	2	3	
1.	marvelous	fantastic	wonderful	[2]
2.	tomorrow	popular	quality	[1]
3.	example	commercial	hospital	[3]
4.	possible	horrible	important	[3]
5.	apartment	Washington	officer	[1]

Before or after this exercise, students should practice the words. Tap or clap to show the stress pattern, if necessary.
● •• marvelous, horrible, popular, wonderful, quality, Washington, possible, hospital, officer
• ● • commercial, fantastic, example, tomorrow, exactly, important, apartment

UNIT 10 ɔ (ball)

Sound production

See Overview, page 5.

Variation   Some people, especially in the western United States and Canada, use the sound ɑ instead of ɔ in some or most of the words practiced in this unit. Note, however, that even speakers who use the sound ɑ elsewhere generally use ɔ before an *r*. British speakers may use a different vowel – ɒ – in some of the words in this unit.

Student difficulties   Many students have difficulty with the sound ɔ, usually making it too short and often confusing it with ɑ, ʌ, or ow, creating confusion among words like *caught, cot, cut,* and *coat*. Speakers of some languages, including Greek, French, German, Turkish, Russian, Spanish, and Japanese, are likely to replace both ɔ and ow with a pure o vowel. Many of these students, as well as others, such as speakers of Arabic, Farsi, Chinese, Dutch, and Indian languages, may also confuse ɔ with ɑ and/or ʌ. (Substituting ɑ may be the least serious problem, since some native speakers also use ɑ instead of ɔ in many words like *caught*.)

If students substitute ɑ or ʌ for ɔ, it may be helpful to focus on the tongue position, telling them to put their tongues back. For students who substitute a pure o, part of the problem may be length; tell them to make the sound longer, and demonstrate the sound, exaggerating its length.

Confusions caused by spelling often contribute to problems with ɔ. The sound ɔ is usually spelled with the letters *o, a, au,* or *aw*. In many languages the letter *o* represents a pure o vowel sound, *a* represents a vowel similar to ɑ, and *au* represents either the sound aw or ow. Students may carry these habits over into English – for example, pronouncing the word *automatic* with the vowel ow or aw. (See also under Spelling in this unit.)

Suggested procedures

Practice 1 and 2   See Overview, pages 6–7.
Contrasts for further practice relevant to student difficulties:
ɑ/ɔ collar/caller, odd/awed, pond/pawned, nod/ gnawed, are/or, ah/awe, tot/taught, farm/form, barn/born, car/core

ʌ/ɔ color/caller, done/dawn, sung/song, fun/fawn, lunch/launch, tuck/talk, stuck/stalk, hunt/haunt, but/bought, gun/gone

Test See Overview, pages 7–8. *Answers:*
1. dawn 2. far 3. cord 4. boss 5. cut
6. color.

Practice 3 See Overview, page 8. (Both the words in the list and the captions for the illustration are from the dialogue that follows.)
  Note: Check stress in compounds such as the following (main stress on the first element, lighter stress on the second):
airport, football, football game, football players, scoreboard, halfback, quarterback, sports report(er).

Dialogue See Overview, pages 8–9. To introduce the situation, call attention to the illustration and the title of the dialogue. If necessary, briefly discuss American football (see illustration), contrasting it with "European football" (known in the United States as *soccer* sɑkər).
Note:
  Pronunciation of *on*: ɑn or ɔn
  Pronunciation of *or*: weak (unstressed) form ər

Stress and intonation In normal (or neutral) English sentence stress (for example, at the beginning of a conversation), the main stress and intonation change are usually on the last important (content) word in the sentence. When a person wants to emphasize something or make a contrast with something said before, however, the main stress and intonation change go on the new idea – the information that contrasts with what was said before.
  The practice in English of varying the placement of the main stress in a sentence to indicate contrast or emphasis is difficult for many students. In some languages, contrast or emphasis is usually signaled by grammatical constructions or by changes in word order rather than by stress. In other languages, although stress is used to show contrast and emphasis, not all the features marking stress in English – higher pitch, greater length, loudness, a clearer vowel – are present as part of stress. Speakers of these languages may not make stressed syllables sound

prominent enough or distinct enough from the surrounding syllables. For speakers of tone languages, such as Chinese or Vietnamese, the use of tone (or pitch) as part of stress and as capable of being varied to express emphasis or feeling may be quite alien.
  Have students listen to and repeat the examples in the Student's Book and read the explanation below the examples. Ask them where the strong stress is in each of B's responses (and why). Students should be able to indicate what the stressed word contrasts with (e.g., in the first example, *football* contrasts with *baseball*).

Conversation Students practice in pairs, as in the example. Check stress and intonation; make sure students understand why the strong stress goes where it does (e.g., in the example, *reporter's* contrasts with *football player's*).

Spelling The spellings *au* and *aw* are regular spellings for the sound ɔ. Two other frequent spellings for the sound – *o* and *a* – commonly spell other sounds. The letter *o* is a common spelling for the sounds ɑ and ow. The letter *a* is a common spelling for the sounds æ, ey, and ɑ; note that it is likely to have the sound ɔ only before the letter *l* (*fall*) or after *w* or *qu* (*water, quarter*).

Further practice

1. Contrastive stress: Sketch a picture of a large ball on the blackboard to elicit from the students, "It's a **large ball**" (normal sentence stress, with main stress on the noun). Then sketch a much smaller ball to elicit, "It's a **small ball**" (contrastive stress, with main stress on the adjective). Sketch other pictures, such as small dog/large dog, large box/small box, tall man/short man, long piece of chalk/short piece of chalk.

2. Ask student volunteers to go to the blackboard. Have each sketch items such as those below. Give each student the description of the item on a piece of paper that other students can't see. Other students then say what the picture is:

a tall glass with a little water in it
a long box with a lot of small balls in it
a long wall with a small door in it
a large house with four small windows and a door
a store with four tall men in it

Linking pronunciation with other course work

Tie pronunciation in with practice of:

1. The greeting "Good morning";

2. Telling the time using *quarter to/quarter past*;

3. Describing people and things using the words *large/small, tall/short, long/short*.

Word stress practice

See Overview, pages 11–12.
Recognition Test: A ● •   B • ●

1. report [B]	6. August [A]
2. repeat [B]	7. awful [A]
3. morning [A]	8. surprised [B]
4. always [A]	9. quarter [A]
5. because [B]	10. returned [B]

UNIT 11 OW (no)

Sound production

See Overview, page 5.

Variation   Length: See note in Unit 1. Compare *road/wrote, close* (verb)/*close* (adj.), *robe/rope*.

British English: British speakers use the sound əʊ instead of ow. The sound əʊ is always a diphthong.

Student difficulties   Students often use a pure vowel o for English ow, leaving out the sec-

ond, gliding part of the vowel. Many students also make the vowel too short. In some cases, their pronunciation of this vowel will be noticeable as part of a "foreign accent" but will not interfere with understanding. In other cases, however, confusion with other vowels may result. Speakers of some languages, such as Spanish, German, French, Dutch, and Japanese, may replace both ow and ɔ with a pure o, leading to confusion between pairs like *caught* and *coat*. Other students, including speakers of Arabic, Chinese, Greek, Italian, Swahili, and West African languages, may also (or instead) substitute a pure o for the ɑ in words like *not*, leading to confusion between pairs like *not* and *note*. Students also confuse ow and ʌ, especially those who pronounce ow too short (for example, speakers of Greek, Arabic, Hebrew, and Polish). Scandinavians may also have difficulty with ow, sometimes confusing it with uw or aw.

Emphasizing the change in mouth position in pronouncing the two parts of the sound ow is helpful for students who substitute a pure vowel o for it. Show how the lips are gradually pushed into a circle as the jaw moves from the half open position of o to the nearly closed position of w. Students can check their own pronunciation using a mirror. Practice the sound first in places where ow is longest and the gliding movement is most noticeable: in stressed syllables at the end of a word (as in *go, below*) or before a voiced consonant (as in *phone, goes*). (In an unstressed syllable, there may be no glide at all.) If any students make the second part of the sound too strong, write the w as a small superscript letter: oᵂ.

Suggested procedures

Practice 1   See Overview, pages 6–7.
Contrasts for further practice relevant to student difficulties:

ɔ/ow   walk/woke, called/cold, jaw/Joe, law/low, chalk/choke, call/coal, fawn/phone, cost/coast, raw/row, Paul/pole, fall/foal, bald/bold, lawn/loan

ʌ/ow   cut/coat, nut/note, come/comb, fun/phone, must/most, but/boat, none/known, sun/sewn, does/doze, gull/goal, rub/robe, hum/home, rust/

roast, dumb/dome, bun/bone, flood/flowed, suck/soak

a/ow cot/coat, John/Joan, want/won't, not/note, hop/hope, calm/comb, sock/soak, rod/road, rob/robe, got/goat, rot/wrote, odd/owed, holly/holy

Note: In practicing the a/ow contrast, call students' attention to the contrast in spelling patterns for these sounds in pairs like *not/note, cot/coat, hopping/hoping.*

Test   See Overview, pages 7–8. *Answers:*
1. hall   2. sew   3. ball   4. woke   5. cold.

Practice 2   See Overview, page 8.
Other words from the dialogue with the sound ow: go, going, know, only, snowball

Dialogue   See Overview, pages 8–9.
Introduce the situation. If students do not live in a region where it snows, you may want to set the scene for the dialogue by showing a picture of snow or by having a brief discussion. Ask, for example: "Have you ever seen snow? Where? What time of year?" "What months of the year does it usually snow in New York/Montreal/Alaska/California/Chile/Australia/etc.?"

Practice 3   This activity provides practice with sound – spelling patterns. The words in the list all contain spellings that commonly represent the sound ow. These spellings may also, however, represent other sounds, as they do in some of the words here. The activity calls students' attention both to regular spellings for the sound ow and to some common words that look like they would be pronounced with ow but are not.

Steps:

1. Make sure students understand the idea of rhyming (in words that rhyme, the last stressed vowel and the sounds that follow it are the same). If necessary, provide or elicit a few examples, using students' names or familiar words that rhyme. Make sure students know that they need to focus on sounds rather than on spellings.

2. Tell students that some of the words in the list have the vowel ow and some words have dif-ferent vowels. Students listen and repeat as you read the words or play the Cassette.

3. Tell students that two words in the list rhyme with the word *sun*, two words rhyme with *Joan*, one word rhymes with *how*, etc.

4. Students write the words from the list that rhyme with the word heading each column. Have students check their answers in pairs, or ask a student to write the answers on the blackboard.

Answers: *sun:* done, one; *Joan:* phone, groan; *how:* now; *no:* snow, throw, know; *gum:* come, some; *Rome:* home

If students have difficulty with the contrast between the sounds ʌ and ow or aw and ow, they may need extra practice. See ʌ/ow contrasts under Practice 1 above and ow/aw contrasts in Unit 17.

Rhyming crossword   Students do the crossword in class, working alone or in pairs, or at home (answers can later be checked with another student). The answers are words that rhyme with the clues but that, unlike most crosswords, do not have the same meanings.

Answers:
Across 1. lonely 3. won't 6. no
   7. so *or* go 8. pillow
Down 1. low 2. yellow 4. on 5. no
   7. so *or* go

Spelling   The spelling patterns for the sounds a and ow often cause confusion. Compare common spelling patterns for these sounds using the letter *o*.

Note: Before two consonants *o* normally has the sound a. But it is a common spelling for the sound ow: before *ll* at the end of a word (*roll*), and before *l* and another consonant in the middle or at the end of a word (*soldier, cold*).

Review: Students say which sound – Sound 1 (ow) or Sound 2 (a) – the letter *o* has in each of the following words.

1. told   6. only
2. clock   7. woke
3. joking   8. bottle
4. don't   9. popular
5. college   10. open

Linking pronunciation with other course work

Tie pronunciation in with practice in:

1. Asking people where they are going and replying to this question (present or future meaning); for example, using a short dialogue such as this:

A: Hello!
B: Hello!
A: Where are you going? Are you going home?
B: No. I'm going *_____.
A: Oh!
B: Where are *you* going? Are *you* going home?
A: No. I'm going *_____.
*Students substitute phrases, for example:

to the post office	to Joe's house
to make a phone call	bowling
to the movies	shopping
to the store	for a walk

2. Negative short answers: "No, I don't/No, I won't."

3. Rejoinders expressing opinion: "I hope so/I think so/I suppose so/I hope not/I don't think so."

Word stress practice

See Overview, pages 11–12.
- ● • window, only, yellow, minutes, pillow, over, lonely, crossword
- • ● ago, hello, across, below

UNIT 12 ʊ (book)

Sound production

See Overview, page 5.
   Students who pronounce ʊ as a sound close to uw might start by practicing uw. Give students the following instructions: "Practice the sound uw. Then put your tongue a *little* lower and relax your lips a little. uw is a long sound; ʊ is a

shorter and more relaxed sound. Do not push your lips forward into a tight circle as you say it."

Variation Length: See note in Unit 2. Dialect variation: See note in Unit 13.

Student difficulties Many students have difficulty distinguishing the sounds ʊ (*foot*) and uw (*boot*). Those likely to have particular difficulty include speakers of French, Italian, Spanish, Portuguese, Chinese, Farsi, and African languages. These languages have only one vowel in the area of ʊ and uw – a pure vowel u. Students tend to substitute this pure vowel for both ʊ and uw, causing confusion between words like *pull/pool* and *look/Luke*. Other students who may have some difficulty include speakers of Dutch, Scandinavian languages, and Japanese; they may confuse ʊ with uw or with other vowels, such as ʌ. Japanese students may pronounce ʊ as a very quiet, whispered sound in some words, often giving the impression that they are dropping the sound altogether.

   In this unit, ʊ is contrasted with another vowel, ɔ, with which it is sometimes confused. Students should try to make ʊ short, in contrast with ɔ, which is long; this should help them later to distinguish ʊ from uw. (See Unit 13 for practice of ʊ versus uw.)

Suggested procedures

Practice 1 See Overview, pages 6–7.
   Contrasts for further practice relevant to student difficulties:

ɔ/ʊ wall/wool, hawk/hook
ʌ/ʊ luck/look, tuck/took, buck/book, putt/put

Test See Overview, pages 7–8. *Answers:*
1. talk 2. bull 3. wool 4. full 5. Paul.

Practice 2 See Overview, page 8.
   Other words from the dialogue that may have the sound ʊ: sure, could (pronunciation: when stressed, kʊd; when unstressed, often kəd).

Note: Many people pronounce *room* (as in *bedroom, living room*) with the sound uw rather than ʊ. Students should follow the pronunciation of their teacher.

Dialogue   See Overview, pages 8–9.

Note:

1. Check that students make the contrast ɔ/ʊ practiced earlier in: *a lost book; Paula Cook; a walk in the woods.*

2. Some students may have particular difficulty with ʊ after the sound w and may omit the w or pronounce it as another sound (as v or sometimes as g).

Negative questions   Negative questions are used for various purposes. People often use negative questions when they expect the answer to be "yes."

Negative questions almost always use a contraction of an auxiliary verb + *not.* Students often have difficulty with the pronunciation, especially in contractions where -*n't* comes after a d, as in *couldn't, shouldn't, wouldn't, didn't,* and *hadn't.* They frequently omit the d or insert a vowel between the d and n. The n here is a "syllabic n," with no vowel before it: kʊdnt. To make this sound, the tongue goes to the roof of the mouth to produce d, but no air is released from the mouth. The tongue stays in the same place to make n, and the air for both sounds escapes through the nose as n is pronounced.

The intonation for a negative question is usually the same (rising) as for an ordinary yes/no question, though it may differ somewhat, depending on the purpose of the question or the attitude of the speaker. Negative questions may start on a high tone, fall, and then rise at the end, or they may end with a falling tone. In practicing, however, students should use just one intonation pattern.

Students listen to and repeat the negative questions in their books, repeating after the Cassette or the teacher. Check their pronunciation of *shouldn't, couldn't,* and *wouldn't* (e.g., to check for silent *l*). Then have students practice in pairs, as in the example, making negative questions for A that could be answered by B's responses.

Spelling   Confusion between the sounds ʊ and uw is no doubt increased by spelling, since both sounds are usually written with the letters *oo* or *u*. The spelling *oo*, in particular, looks as if it should be a long sound, encouraging students to substitute uw for ʊ. Note, too, that in many languages the letter *u* is the spelling for a pure tense vowel u, which students may use in place of both ʊ and uw in English. The letter *u* is also a common spelling in English for the sound ʌ, which also is sometimes confused with ʊ.

The spelling *oo* is likely to be pronounced ʊ before the letters *d, t,* and *k* (this rule is not foolproof; exceptions include *food, blood,* and *flood*). The spelling *u* is likely to be pronounced ʊ before *ll* and *sh* (exceptions include *dull* and *rush*).

Further practice

Students make sentences from the blackboard that are appropriate to the teacher's oral cues:
Blackboard:

(Don't) Put your foot on the	brake
	accelerator
	clutch

Teacher's cues:
I want to start the car/stop the car/change gear/go up a hill/go down a hill/go faster/go slower/pass another car.
Note: brake breyk; accelerator əksɛləreytər; clutch klʌtʃ.

Linking pronunciation with other course work

Tie pronunciation in with practice of:

1. Modal auxiliaries *could/couldn't, should/shouldn't, would/wouldn't;*

2. Tag questions using *should, would,* and *could.* For example, give students negative statements; they make and answer tag questions, practicing in pairs:
Example: He couldn't cook.

A: He couldn't cook, could he?
B: No, he couldn't.

3. Expressions using the word *good*; for example: "Good morning/afternoon/night." "Have a good weekend/time/trip/vacation/evening."

Word stress practice

Practice compounds that have a strong stress on the first syllable and a lighter stress on the last syllable.

- • football, bookshelf, cookbook, bedroom, bathroom, somewhere, scoreboard, snowball, crossword, bookstore
- • • living room, dining room, anywhere, everywhere

UNIT 13 uw (boot)

Sound production

See Overview, page 5.

Variation   Length: See note in Unit 1. Compare *lose/loose*, *use* (verb)/*use* (noun), *prove/proof*, *sued/suit*, *rude/root* (or *route*).

Dialect variation: In a few words, including *room*, *broom*, *groom*, *roof*, *hoof*, *root*, and *soot*, the spelling *oo* is pronounced with the sound uw by some people and ʊ by others.

Student difficulties   Many students confuse the sounds ʊ and uw (see Unit 12, under Student Difficulties and Spelling). Although most students replace both sounds with a pure vowel u that sounds more like uw, speakers of some languages, such as Greek, Russian, Polish, and Turkish, may use a shorter or more relaxed vowel resembling ʊ. Japanese students tend to pronounce uw without rounding the lips, which gives it a different sound. Scandinavians and Turks may also sometimes have difficulty with uw.

Emphasize that uw is a long sound and that ʊ

is not. If necessary, write the sound contrast words (Practice 1) on the blackboard:
look   Luuuuke
pull   pooool
To stress the length and the rounding of the lips, it may be helpful to tell students to say uw twice or to round their lips twice. Note that, unlike uw, ʊ is a short vowel and does not come at the end of words. Compare uw and ʊ in *too full*, *two books*, *new wool*.

Suggested procedures

Practice 1   See Overview, pages 6–7.
Note: There are few common sound contrast pairs that contrast ʊ and uw. (The words *foot* and *boot*, used here to contrast the sounds, are obviously not a minimal pair.)

Soot is the black powder or dust produced from burning that sticks to the sides of chimneys.

Contrasts for further practice: *hood/who'd*, *could/cooed*, *should/shoed*.

Test   See Overview, pages 7–8. *Answers:*
1. "Pull"   2. Luke   3. suit.

Practice 2   See Overview, page 8.
Note:

1. The words *music* and *usual* have the sound yuw (rather than just uw). Some people also use the pronunciation yuw in other words here: Tuesday, student, introduce, newspaper, Happy New Year.

2. Pronunciation of *you*: see below, under Stress.

Dialogue   See Overview, pages 8–9.
If necessary, explain the greeting "Happy New Year." Ask, "Which day of the year do people say 'Happy New Year'?"
Steps:

1. Students listen to the conversations on the Cassette or read by the teacher, with their books open.

2. With books closed, students listen again. Stop

the Cassette after the first person in each conversation has spoken. Students try to remember what the second person said.

Note: Make sure students pronounce the word *good* with the sound ʊ rather than uw.

Extension Discuss ways of celebrating New Year's Day in different countries or different practices associated with New Year's, such as making New Year's resolutions, making predictions about the coming year, or eating special foods.

Stress Students listen to and repeat questions and answers from the dialogue.

Note: In A's questions, the word *you* is not stressed and may have the sound yə. The unstressed words *do you* in a question may be pronounced də yə or, in very rapid speech (at the beginning of a question), dyə. In B's questions, *you* is stressed and has the sound yuw.

Conversation Working in pairs, students make up a question for A that could be followed by B's response. Ask pairs of students to say some of their conversations when they are finished. Make sure that B puts stress on the word *you* when it is being used for the second time in the conversation (as, probably, in 5, 6, 7).

Spelling Review spellings with the letters *u* and *oo*: Give students a list of words such as the one that follows. Students group the words according to the vowel sound spelled with the letters *u* or *oo*: good, soon, cook, blood, afternoon, look, student, put, full, June, just, introduce, study.

	Sound 1 (ʊ)	*Sound 2* (uw)	*Sound 3* (ʌ)
Example:	book	boot	cup

Answers:
Sound 1 (ʊ) good, cook, look, put, full
Sound 2 (uw) soon, afternoon, student, June, introduce
Sound 3 (ʌ) blood, just, study

Further practice

Students practice dialogues that use the sounds ʊ and uw. Examples:

1. A: Do you like *_____ ?
   B: Yes, I do.
   A: I like *_____ too.
*Substitute:

cooking	fruit
football	school
sugar	blue shoes
bookstores	movies
books	grapefruit juice

The words in the first column have the sound ʊ, and the words in the second column have uw. Practice the words from the blackboard first. Then practice the question, giving cues. For example:
TEACHER: Football
STUDENT: Do you like football?
Students then practice the dialogue in pairs.

2. Use the same procedures as above for this dialogue:
A: Excuse me.
B: Yes?
A: Do you know where I could get some good ¹_____ ?
B: Yes. There's a place next to the ²_____ that has very good ¹_____. I'm going there too.
Substitute words from column 1 in blanks marked 1, words from column 2 in blanks marked 2.

1	2
shoes	supermarket
wool	bookstore
boots	swimming pool
cookies	butcher
toothpaste	movie theater
cookbooks	shoe store
fruit juice	newspaper stand

(*Note:* Sound uw in shoes, boots, toothpaste, fruit juice, supermarket, pool, movie, newspaper; sound ʊ in wool, cookies, cookbooks, bookstore, butcher.)

Linking pronunciation with other course work

Tie pronunciation in with practice of:

1. Short answers or tag questions using *do* (simple present tense);

2. Questions beginning with *who* or *whose;*

3. Introductions. For example:
STUDENT A: B, this is C./B, I'd like you to meet
            C.
STUDENT B: How do you do?/Nice to meet you.
(Note falling intonation in "How do you do?")

4. Compliments. For example:
STUDENT A: I like your *_____. (Are they/Is it
            new?)
            or
            Those are/that's a nice *_____.
STUDENT B: Thank you.

*Substitute: shoes, glasses, boots, coat, shirt, bag, hat, dress, socks, etc.

(Note that compliments often have a rather high intonation before the fall at the end.)

Word stress practice

Students listen to the following pairs and tell whether the stress pattern for the two words or phrases is the same or different.

1. introduce/afternoon [S]
2. thank you/Peru [D]
3. confuse/music [D]
4. newspaper/example [D]
5. Happy New Year/ conversation [S – for most people]
6. cousin/movie [S]
7. student/party [S]
8. Tuesday/confuse [D]
9. introduce/New Year's Eve [S]

UNIT 14 Review

This unit provides additional practice and review of the vowels ʌ, ɑ, ɔ, ow, ʊ, uw, and ə. The set of words with contrasting vowels is not on the Cassette. Before proceeding, you may want to have students listen to and repeat some or all of these words, reading across, or reading first down and then across.

Listening practice

Students write down or say aloud the number of the vowel that they hear in each word as it is said by the teacher or recorded on the Cassette. *Answers:* oh!; pool; full; law; done; lock; look; pole; luck; fool.

Pronunciation practice

The phrases in this exercise contain the sound ə in the weak, unstressed forms of the words shown in the left column, as well as the vowels practiced in Units 7 through 13. Students listen to and repeat the phrases in the right column as pronounced on the Cassette or by the teacher. Make sure students do not put stress on the weak forms.

Other words from the dialogue with these sounds: just, nothing, sometimes, Don, got, Dawn, fall, water, all, talk, awfully, no, know, cold, don't, those, oh, pushed, pulled, good, couldn't, foolish, Lucas, two, too, shoes, fooling, stupid, ooh, around, but, was, into, because, ugh, uh, huh, everyone, on.

Dialogue

See Overview, pages 8–9.

Puzzle

Students circle or say the word in each group that does not have the same vowel sound as the other words. Go over the example. Emphasize that they need to focus on sounds, not spellings.

Students can work in pairs or groups. Check the answers at the end, using the numbers for the sounds from the Listening Practice at the beginning of the unit (e.g., "Which sound does the word *joking* have?" "Which sound do the other words have?").

Answers: 1. joking (Sound 4) 2. look (Sound 5) 3. closed (Sound 4) 4. food (Sound 6) 5. love (Sound 1) 6. cold (Sound 4).

Spelling review

1. Give students a list of words, on paper or the blackboard, that have the sounds practiced in Units 7 through 13. Students sort the words by sound, grouping words with the same vowel sound together. (See additional instructions in Unit 6.) Sample list of words, to be given in scrambled order:

ʌ   love, nothing, cousin, does, funny
ɑ   job, shopping, father, problem, bottle
ɔ   fall, thought, awful, lost, walk
ow   cold, won't, throw, coat, over
ʊ   should, woman, took, push, wood
uw   movie, you, Tuesday, suit, shoes

2. To review these or other spelling patterns, use a list of rhyming words as the basis for a game of *Concentration* (matching pairs), in which the object is to find pairs of words that rhyme. The game gives students practice with the use of different spellings to represent a single sound (as, for example, in *sun, touch, blood*) and with the use of the same spelling to represent different sounds (as in *love, stove, move*). Both ideas are often difficult for students who speak languages in which spelling is more or less phonetic and a single sound usually has a single spelling.

To prepare the game, write each word on a small card, using about twenty to thirty words (ten to fifteen pairs). To play, the cards are shuffled and turned face down. A student turns two cards face up and says the words on them. (Other players should be able to see the cards, to check the student's pronunciation and judgment as to whether the words rhyme.) If the words rhyme, the student keeps the cards and turns over another pair. If the words do not rhyme, the student puts the cards face down in their original places and the next student follows the

same procedure. The player who accumulates the most pairs is the winner. The game can be played using one large set of cards for the whole class or with separate sets of cards distributed to groups of students.

Sample list of matching pairs:

ow	ʌ	aw
stone/groan	sun/done	how/now
know/sew	much/touch	loud/crowd
stove/drove	love/glove	
home/comb	gum/some	
	mud/blood	

ʊ	uw
good/could	move/prove
wool/full	food/rude

Word stress recognition test

See Overview, pages 11–12.
A ● •   B • ●
1. foolish [A]
2. sometimes [A]
3. because [B]
4. nothing [A]
5. review [B]
6. around [B]
7. fooling [A]
8. sudden [A]
9. stupid [A]
10. belong [B]

UNIT 15 ay (fine)

Sound production

See Overview, page 5.
Note: Some people say the second part of **ay** more like the sound **ɪ**.

Variation The exact sounds making up the diphthong **ay** may vary. Some people say the first part as a sound between **ɑ** and **æ**. Other people, especially Canadians and people living in the northern United States, pronounce the first sound more like **ʌ**, especially when this diphthong comes before a voiceless consonant, as in *like* (lʌyk).

The word *I* is often pronounced just as the vowel ɑ, especially when it is unstressed or used in contractions like *I'll* or *I'm*. Many speakers in the U.S. South tend to drop the second element of this diphthong, especially before a consonant. Length: See note in Unit 1. Compare: *ride/right, eyes/ice, live* (adj.)/*life, hide/height*.

Student difficulties   Most students have little difficulty with the sound ay. Some students, for example speakers of Spanish, Russian, and Scandinavian languages, may make the second part of the diphthong too strong, giving the two elements in the diphthong equal weight. For these students, it may be helpful to write the symbol for the sound on the blackboard as aʸ, with the y shown as a small superscript letter. French and Italian speakers may either make the second element too strong or drop it altogether. Chinese speakers may make both sounds too short and indistinct. Other students who may have difficulty with the sound ay include speakers of Arabic, Swahili, and Thai. Students who have difficulty commonly substitute the first vowel alone or confuse ay with ey or ɔy. Vietnamese speakers may drop final consonants after this or other diphthongs.

Suggested procedures

Practice 1   See Overview, pages 6–7.
   Contrasts for further practice relevant to student difficulties:
æ/ay had/hide, laugh/life, man/mine, fan/fine, sad/side, am/I'm, sand/signed, rat/right, bat/bite, fat/fight, mat/might, lamb/lime, as/eyes, dad/died, sat/sight, add/I'd, lack/like, tap/type, dam/dime, clam/climb, pan/pine, flat/flight
ey/ay A/I, lake/like, late/light, May/my, tray/try, wait/white, bake/bike

Test   See Overview, pages 7–8. *Answers:*
1. back   2. vine   3. cat   4. had   5. height.

Practice 2   See Overview, page 8.
   Other words from the dialogue with the sound ay: hi, by, buy, nice, time, Friday, Mike, Brian, Simon, all right, ice cream, I'm, typing.

Dialogue   See Overview, pages 8–9.

1. Check students' understanding of vocabulary, according to their level. For example, ask them to find a word in the dialogue that means:
   a ride in a car
   an insect with many legs
   a noun that means "quiet"
   a machine for writing
   a person who uses this machine as a job
   the activity of using this machine (a verb)

2. Students ask and answer questions like the following, filling in the blanks with the names Mike, Myra, and Violet.
   Does ___ like ___ ?
   Is ___ nice to ___ ?
   How does ___ probably feel?

Conversation   Students should practice the *-ing* forms first (note stress in the column on the right: strong stress on the first word, weaker stress on the second). Read the dialogue, either by yourself or with a student. Students practice the dialogue in pairs, switching roles.
   Note: Sometimes is pronounced with strong stress on *some*. In *some other time*, *some* is pronounced as unstressed səm. *Would you* is often pronounced wʊdʒə in rapid speech.

Adding *-ing*   Spelling rules for adding *-ing*:

1. Verbs that end in silent *e* drop the *e* before adding *-ing*: ride – riding.

2. Verbs of one syllable that end in *ie* change the *ie* to *y* before adding *-ing*: lie – lying. (Verbs that end in *y* do not change: fly – flying, buy – buying, say – saying, carry – carrying.)

3. Verbs that end in a single vowel letter followed by a single consonant letter, with the vowel pronounced with strong stress, double the consonant before adding *-ing*: swim – swimming, begin – beginning. (Exception: the consonant *x* is never doubled: fix – fixing.)

4. Other verbs do not change before adding *-ing*: fight – fighting, fish – fishing.
Steps:

1. Students practice saying the verbs. Tell them to listen to the vowel sound and look at the

spelling. Students say which words have the sound **ay** and which have the sound **ɪ**.

2. Students practice saying the *-ing* forms.

3. Use the blackboard to demonstrate any of the spelling rules above that you want to discuss (e.g., rid*é* – riding).

4. Students fill in the spaces in the chart.

Call attention to the difference in spelling between *-ing* verbs pronounced with the sound **ɪ** and the sound **ay**. A word spelled with a single stressed *i* followed by a single consonant (and *-ing*) will have the sound **ay**. If the word has two consonants after the vowel, the *i* has the sound **ɪ**. (Exceptions: The consonants *x* and *v* will not give a clue as to how the vowel is pronounced, since these consonants are never doubled.) Write a few words with *-ing* on the blackboard (e.g., *dining, admitting*); students try pronouncing them.

Spelling   The spelling patterns for the sounds **ay** and **ɪ** often cause confusion. Compare pairs of words such as the following to call attention to the difference in spelling patterns for these sounds using the letter *i*:
bit – bite, hid – hide, fin – fine, pin – pine, dim – dime, rid – ride
lit – light, fit – fight
dinner – diner, filling – filing

Linking pronunciation with other course work

Tie pronunciation in with practice of:

1. Talking about likes and dislikes; for example: "I like/don't like/don't mind ice cream/pineapple/rice/fried rice/wine/pie/wide ties/mice/this exercise."

2. Offering things using "Would you like . . ."; for example: "Would you like some ice cream?"

3. Talking about the future using the present progressive; for example: "What are you doing tonight/on Friday/Saturday night/this weekend/

for vacation?" "I'm staying home/going to the library/seeing friends."

4. Expressions with *go* + *-ing* verb (gerund); for example: go hiking/go shopping/go dancing/go bowling/go swimming/go fishing/go skiing/go boating/go jogging/go camping/go mountain climbing. Talk about what students like or don't like doing, activities they've done, or future plans.

Word stress practice

Read the following words. Have students mark the syllable that has the strongest stress in each word, by drawing a line under the syllable or by putting an accent mark over the stressed vowel. Students should practice the words either before or after doing this.

1. typing	8. good-bye
2. never	9. silence
3. sometimes	10. typewriter
4. library	11. Friday
5. tonight	12. maybe
6. typist	13. spider
7. behind	14. all right

UNIT 16   ɔy (boy)

Sound production

See Overview, page 5.
   Note: Some people say the second part of ɔy ƆY more like the sound **ɪ**. ɪ

Variation   Some people, particularly in the South of the United States, tend to drop the second part of this diphthong, especially before a consonant.

Student difficulties   Students who may have difficulty with this sound include speakers of Arabic, Farsi, French, Indian languages, Swahili, and Thai. Such students commonly substitute either the first element alone (ɔ) or the sound **ay**, for example, saying *all* or *isle* in place of *oil*. Speakers of some languages, such as Spanish, Italian, Dutch, and Scandinavian languages, may have a tendency to make the second element too strong; for these students it may be helpful to write the symbol for the sound on the blackboard as ɔ^y, showing the second element as a small, superscript letter. Other students, such as Lao, Vietnamese, and to a lesser extent Khmer speakers, tend to drop any final consonant after a diphthong. Many students find ɔy hardest to pronounce when it is followed by l, as in *boil*.

Suggested procedures

Practice 1   See Overview, pages 6–7.
  Contrasts for further practice relevant to student difficulties:
ɔ/ɔy tall/toil, fall/foil, call/coil, pause or paws/poise, saw/soy
ay/ɔy buy/boy, tie/toy, pint/point, isle/oil, file/foil, tile/toil, liar/lawyer, fire/foyer, kind/coined, lied/Lloyd, vice/voice, pies/poise, lighter/loiter, rise/Roy's, rye/Roy

Test   See Overview, pages 7–8. *Answers:*
1. oil   2. bald   3. raw   4. boiling.

Practice 2   See Overview, page 8.
  Other words from the dialogue with the sound ɔy: noisy, noisiest.
Note:

1. Some students may pronounce the letter *s* in *noisy*, *noise*, or *boys* as the sound s instead of z.

2. Some students may pronounce the *-ed* in *annoyed* or *spoiled* as an extra syllable. Write these words on the blackboard, and erase or draw a line through the *e* to show that it is not pronounced. Write the words *enjoyed* and *destroyed*; students try pronouncing them.

3. For students who confuse ay and ɔy, check their pronunciation of *buy* contrasted with *boy*.

Dialogue   See Overview, pages 8–9.

Stress   In English, only the important words in a sentence are stressed. The unimportant words,

like articles (*a, the*), prepositions (*in, of, at*, etc.), and auxiliary verbs (*have, been, will, do*, etc.), are usually not stressed. Stressed syllables in English are not just louder, they also take longer to say and are often said at a higher pitch. Unstressed syllables are not just quieter, they also are shorter, and often have a reduced (unclear) vowel sound (often ə). The difference between stressed and unstressed syllables in English tends to be greater than in many other languages (e.g., Spanish, Italian, and Japanese). English is also a "stress-timed" language. This means that stressed syllables tend to occur at regularly spaced intervals, regardless of the number of intervening unstressed syllables. The amount of time it takes to say a sentence depends mostly on the number of stressed syllables it has rather than on its total number of syllables. The more unstressed syllables there are between stressed syllables, the more rapidly they are said.

  Many students have difficulty both with reducing vowels and with stress timing. Many languages, including Spanish, Italian, and Japanese, are "syllable-timed." In syllable-timed languages, all syllables take about the same amount of time to say and tend to follow each other at more or less regular intervals. There is no squashing together of unstressed syllables between much more prominent stressed syllables. When speakers of syllable-timed languages transfer their native language rhythms to English, it can create problems both in being understood and, especially, in understanding others. They tend to pronounce words that should be unstressed and reduced, like *and, but, as, at, from*, and *have*, with stress and full vowels. And they may have difficulty hearing these words at all when they are said by a native English speaker in their unstressed, reduced form.

Steps:

1. Students listen to the sentences in the Student's Book, read by the teacher or as recorded on the Cassette.

2. Students listen again, this time accompanied by the teacher tapping with a ruler or clapping.

3. Students repeat the sentences, while tapping on their desks or clapping. If they have difficulty

with the rhythm, draw variously sized dots on the blackboard to represent the rhythm of each sentence, or write the sentences on the blackboard, using large capitals for stressed syllables and small, squashed-together lowercase letters for the unstressed syllables. The rhythm of the sentences can also be practiced using nonsense syllables: DAH DAH DAH. də DAH DAH DAH. də DAH də DAH DAH.

Spelling The spelling of the sound ɔy is fairly regular. At the end of words it is spelled *oy*. At the beginning or in the middle of words, it can be spelled either *oi* or *oy*, though *oi* is more common.

Further practice

Write a simple two- or three-word sentence on the blackboard (e.g., from other course work). The words should all be of one syllable and stressed (content words). Students then try progressively adding function words to make a set of sentences for stress practice, as in the earlier Stress section.

Linking pronunciation with other course work

Tie pronunciation in with practice in talking about what students enjoy, don't enjoy, or avoid doing; for example: "I enjoy/don't enjoy/avoid hiking/walking/sports/drawing/cooking/driving/noisy parties."

Word stress practice

See Overview, pages 11–12.
Recognition Test: A ●•   B •●   C •●•

1. annoy [B]
2. themselves [B]
3. noisy [A]
4. enjoying [C]
5. destroy [B]
6. maybe [A]
7. annoyed [B]
8. annoying [C]
9. enjoy [B]
10. continue [C]

UNIT 17 aw (house)

Sound production

See Overview, page 5.
   Note: Some people say the second part of **aw** more like the sound ʊ.

Variation The first vowel in the diphthong **aw** may vary in sound. Some people say it more like æ, some more like ɑ, and many use a vowel that is somewhere between these two in quality.
   Canadians often pronounce this diphthong as ʌw before voiceless consonants, as in *house* hʌws or *about* əbʌwt.
   Speakers in the southern United States may tend to drop the second part of the diphthong, pronouncing it as a long ɑ or æ sound.
   Length: See note in Unit 1. Compare: *bowed/bout, house* (verb)/*house* (noun), *mouth* (verb)/*mouth* (noun).

Student difficulties Many students have little difficulty with the sound **aw**. The most common errors are to omit the second part of the diphthong, substituting a sound close to ɑ, or to make the first part of the diphthong too short and the second part too strong. The latter is a common tendency among speakers of French, Italian, Spanish, and Russian. Chinese students may make both sounds too short and indistinct.
   Encourage students who omit the second sound to watch your lips as you say **aw** and to use a mirror when practicing it themselves. For students who make the second sound too strong, write the first vowel in the symbol larger or darker than the second vowel, or tell students to whisper the second sound.

Suggested procedures

Practice 1 See Overview, pages 6–7.
   Contrasts for further practice:

ɑ/aw dot/doubt, spot/spout, fond/found
ow/aw oh!/ow, no/now, phoned/found, load/
  loud, tone/town, a boat/about

Note: Many speakers add the sound ə between
aw and a following r: *hour* awər.

Test   See Overview, pages 7–8. *Answers:*
1. scouts   2. hour   3. Don   4. shots
5. pounds.

Practice 2   See Overview, page 8.

Dialogue   See Overview, pages 8–9.
  Note: The word *our* is often pronounced ɑr.

Stress   In two-word verbs, both words are
stressed (unlike a verb followed by a preposition,
where only the verb would be stressed: "He's
lying on the **floor**"). If there is an object pronoun, as in the second group of sentences, it
does not get stress. Tap or clap to show the
stress if students have difficulty. Note, too, the
occurrence of the "flap" t sound (see Unit 23),
which many students find difficult, at the end of
a word like *it* when the next word begins with a
vowel (e.g., *out*).
  Students listen to and repeat the sentences.
Then they say the sentence that describes each of
the pictures.
  After this exercise, tell students to look at the
dialogue again. Ask them to find a two-word
verb that means:
1. to become calmer or quieter (*calm down*)
2. to remove something or cause something to
leave (*get it out*)

Spelling   At the end of a word, the sound aw
is spelled *ow*. In other positions, it may be
spelled either with *ou* or *ow*. Note that *ow* is also
a common spelling for the sound ow (see
Unit 11).

Further practice

Write questions like the following on the
blackboard:
How far is it from your house to _____ ?
How long does it take to get to _____ by car?

Encourage students to ask the questions using
familiar place names. At first the teacher answers: "about two miles," "about an hour," and
so forth. Then have students answer the
questions.

Linking pronunciation with other course work

Tie pronunciation in with practice of:

1. Questions beginning with the word *how*; for
example, asking people how they get to work or
school and how long it takes; how far away
places are; how much things cost;
2. "How are you?" "How's your sister?" etc.;
3. Questions with *How many/How much*;
4. Two-word verbs.

UNIT 18   Review

This unit provides additional practice and review
of the diphthongs ay, ɔy, and aw. The set of
words with contrasting vowels is not on the Cassette. Before proceeding, you may want to have
students listen to and repeat some or all of these
words, reading across, or reading first down and
then across.

Listening practice

Students write down or say aloud the number of
the vowel that they hear in each word as it is
said by the teacher or recorded on the Cassette.
Answers: lied; toil; bow; boy; tile; oil; loud.

Dialogue

See Overview, pages 8–9.
  Students listen to the dialogue on the Cassette
or read by the teacher, first with their books
closed and again with their books open. They
can then practice the dialogue in pairs, if the

practice seems needed. Finally, students list words from the dialogue that have each of the sounds practiced in Units 15 through 17. Point out that the numbers here (Sounds 1, 2, 3) are the same ones used in the listening practice at the beginning of the unit.

	Sound 1	Sound 2	Sound 3
1.	like	boy	down
2.	lying	Roy	ground
3.	I'm	Joy	brown
4.	trying	oil	cloud
5.	why	enjoy	mountain
6.	buy	pointing	
7.	I		
8.	nice		
9.	behind		
10.	dialogue		

Spelling review

Give students a list of words, on paper or on the blackboard, that have the sounds practiced in Units 11 and 15 through 17. Students sort the words by sound, grouping words with the same vowel sound together. (See additional instructions in Unit 6.) Here is a sample list of words to be given in scrambled order:

ay	high, buy, pint, eye, fly
oy	point, destroy, choice, annoying, noisy
aw	loud, crowd, vowel, thousand, brown
ow	grow, though, sew, snow, know

Word stress recognition test

See Overview, pages 11–12.
A ●•   B •●

1. enjoy [B]	6. behind [B]
2. painting [A]	7. lying [A]
3. noisy [A]	8. around [B]
4. polite [B]	9. good-bye [B]
5. mountain [A]	10. pronounce [B]

UNIT 19 ə Review (a camera)

This unit provides additional practice and review of the sound ə. For notes on Sound Production and Variation, see Unit 8.

Student difficulties

Many students have difficulty with the patterns of word stress in English. Following are descriptions of typical difficulties.

In many languages (e.g., Hungarian, Czech, Farsi, and French), word stress is very predictable, always falling on the same syllable (e.g., the first or the last) in words. To students who speak these languages, English stress may seem chaotic and unpredictable. (The idea that stress can vary according to the meaning or use of a word – as in the different stress patterns that distinguish the noun record from the verb record, for example – may be particularly alien to such students.) Students who speak languages in which word stress is very regular need to know that they must learn the stress pattern of an English word as a basic part of its pronunciation.

In some languages (for example, French), the stress patterns of individual words may be modified when the words occur in phrases. Students who speak these languages need to know that in English the stress pattern of an individual word remains the same when it occurs in a phrase or sentence.

In some languages (e.g., Japanese and Swahili), all or most syllables may be pronounced with almost equal stress – or may sound as if they are to the English speaker, because the features that indicate stress in English (greater force, longer vowel, change in pitch) are not all present in these other languages. If students do not put enough stress on syllables, tell them to make the stressed syllables (shown in darker type in the Student's Book) stronger or more important. Show them that the stressed vowel is lengthened. Use arrows on the blackboard to show the higher pitch of the stressed syllable.

Long words in English often have more than one stress – a strong stress and a weaker stress. Other languages, such as Greek and Russian, may only have one stress per word; speakers of these languages may seem to slur over the syllables with weaker stress in words like **con**ver**sa**tion or **pho**to**graph**.

In many languages, even syllables that are unstressed are pronounced with a full, clear vowel. In English, unstressed syllables are usually pronounced with an indistinct, reduced vowel – usually ə or ɪ. Students who pronounce unstressed syllables with clear vowels may sound to native English speakers as if they are stressing those syllables. In English stressed syllables sound more prominent and unstressed syllables less prominent than in most other languages; the use of reduced vowels contributes greatly to this effect.

Also see Unit 8 for a discussion of general difficulties with the sound ə, and Units 8 and 16 for difficulties with sentence stress and weak forms.

Suggested procedures

Practice 1   Here students practice the stress patterns of individual words. The stress pattern of a word is one of the most important aspects of its pronunciation. Since unstressed syllables often have reduced vowels in English, knowing where the stress is helps to indicate how the vowels should be pronounced. If the stress is put on the wrong syllable, the vowels will probably be given the wrong sounds, and the word may be incomprehensible to an English listener. Write words that cause difficulty on the blackboard. Show syllables that have strong stress in large capitals, syllables with weak stress in smaller capitals, and unstressed syllables in small, lowercase letters written close together. Or, use variously sized dots to represent the stress pattern.

Note that most of the words in the first section of Practice 1 begin with prefixes like *a-*, *be-*, *de-*, *for-*, *pro-*, and *re-*. These word elements, along with others, like *com-* (*complete*), *con-* (*contain*), *im-* (*impress*), *pre-* (*prepare*), and *to-* (*today*), are usually unstressed. A two-syllable word beginning with

one of these elements will generally have stress on the second syllable. Reflexive pronouns (like *herself*) are also stressed on the second syllable.

In the second section of Practice 1, note that *tomorrow* begins with *to-*, which is usually unstressed. *Conversation* ends with *-tion*; words with this ending have stress on the syllable before the *-tion* (see Unit 29).

In the third section of Practice 1, note that words ending in *-er*, *-ful*, *-ly*, *-able*, and usually *-en* or *-et* do not have stress on these syllables.

Discuss these notes, according to the level of the class. It is often helpful for students who find English word stress confusing and unpredictable to have patterns like these pointed out. Write additional words, such as those below, on the blackboard; ask students to try saying the words and to add them to the appropriate section of the list.

often	review	English	pronunciation
about	aloud	under	ticket
picture	mother	between	careful
syllable	questions	happen	deliver

Practice 2 and 3   Students practice stress in phrases and sentences. Just as some syllables in words are stressed and some are unstressed, there are regular patterns of stress in phrases and sentences, with the important words (usually content words) stressed and the unimportant words (usually "grammatical" words) unstressed. Note that in a word of more than one syllable, the syllable that is stressed when the word is in a sentence is the same syllable that gets stress when the word is said by itself.

Students listen to and repeat phrases and then sentences. English sentences tend to have fewer strong stresses than sentences in many other languages; make sure students do not stress too many words. Note that the first three examples in each section have two strong stresses and should therefore be said in about the same length of time. Tap out the strong stresses with a ruler to show the rhythm and the amount of time in which the sentences should be said; have students repeat the sentences accompanied by the teacher tapping. Make sure students do not put stress on the weak (unstressed) forms. After listening and repeating, students should cover the normal spellings on the left and practice questions and answers about the pictures. The respellings on the right show where to use the sound ə.

Reading   Students listen to the reading on the Cassette or read aloud by the teacher. Then students practice reading aloud, giving particular attention to the use of the sound ə, especially in weak forms of words.

Spelling   See Unit 8 for spellings of the sound ə.

Linking pronunciation with other course work

Tie pronunciation in with practice of:

1. Talking about the time: "What's the time?" "It's one o'clock/It's a quarter to six," etc.

2. Weak forms of *and, but, of, at, was, some, to, her,* etc.

UNIT 20   3r *(word)*

Sound production

See Overview, page 5.

Note: Some speakers say the sound 3r with the middle of the tongue raised or bunched up toward the roof of the mouth, without curling the tongue back.

Variation   British speakers use the sound 3, but without a following r sound.

Student difficulties   The sound 3r is difficult for almost all students. They may confuse it with almost any other vowel, often depending on how it is spelled. When the sound is written *er, ir, or,* or *ur* (as in *person, bird, work,* or *nurse*), students are likely to pronounce it with the vowel suggested by the spelling, plus an r sound. 3r

is also often confused with ɑ (especially by Japanese students) or ʌ, so that *burn* may be pronounced like *barn* or *bun*. Some students (e.g., Dutch, Scandinavian, and French speakers) may pronounce the vowel with the lips pushed forward and rounded. Many students have particular difficulty after the sound w, as in *work* or *worst,* or before or after l, as in *girl* or *clerk*.

Note that the tongue position for this sound is basically the same as for the English consonant r. If students can produce an English r, try respelling words on the blackboard omitting the vowel letter, for example "brd" (or "b'rd") and "hr" (or "h'r") for *bird* and *her*. (Even if students have not mastered English r, these respellings will call attention to the fact that there is no distinct, separate vowel sound.)

Students should spend some time on the mouth position for 3r. (Suggestions for practice of r in Units 45 and 46 may also be helpful here.) Note that the lips should be in a neutral position, not rounded. The tongue should be raised toward the hard part of the roof of the mouth (the hard palate); some students pull their tongues too far back.

In teaching this sound, emphasize the fact that 3r has many different spellings, all with the same sound.

Suggested procedures

Practice 1, 2, and 3   See Overview, pages 6–7.

Contrasts for further practice relevant to student difficulties:

ɔr/3r wore/were, born/burn, warm/worm,
    blackboard/blackbird, store/stir, course/curse,
    form/firm, Norse/nurse
ɑr/3r Carl/curl, farm/firm, carton/curtain, dart/dirt
ʌ/3r but/Burt, study/sturdy, fun/fern, cut/curt,
    pus/purse
eər/3r wear/were, hair/her, stair/stir, fair/fur, pair/
    purr

Test   See Overview, pages 7–8. *Answers:*
1. far   2. buds   3. word   4. walk   5. burns
6. gulls.

Practice 4   See Overview, page 8.

Dialogue   See Overview, pages 8–9.

1. Check students' pronunciation of the words *wear, short,* and *ward* to make sure they do not use the sound 3r in these words; contrast these words with *were, shirt,* and *word.*

2. Note that "er," used to represent a sound of hesitation when speaking, can be pronounced in various ways, for example ʌ, ə, and 3 (the *r* is usually silent).

Intonation   This exercise practices tag questions with falling intonation, which are often difficult for students. Students often use rising intonation, either because question tags in their own language use this intonation or simply because the question form leads them to expect that rising intonation would be used. The situation is made more complicated by the fact that tag questions in English often *are* said with rising intonation. This happens when the meaning is closer to a real question – when the speaker is less sure that he or she is right or that the other person will agree. Often, however, the speaker strongly expects or hopes that the other person will agree with or confirm what was said. In cases like this, the speaker is not really asking a question. The person is doing something more like making a comment or giving an opinion and expects confirmation or agreement. Question tags of this type have falling intonation.

Note that the tag questions are said in two intonation groups, both ending with falling intonation. In the first phrase, the main stress is on the last important (content) word, as it is in an ordinary sentence. In the second phrase, the main stress is on the auxiliary verb.

Students practice first the tags and then entire questions, repeating after the Cassette or the teacher. Then students ask and answer questions in pairs, as in the examples. Note that all the statements are negative, so that all the tags will be affirmative.

Spelling   Point out the variety of spellings for the sound 3r. The only vowel letter that is *not* used to represent this sound (at least by itself) is *a.*

For review, give students, on paper or the blackboard, pairs of words like those below. Students indicate which word has the sound 3r.

1. worse, horse   6. short, word
2. heard, heart   7. earn, near
3. fire, first   8. sorry, worry
4. were, there   9. turn, torn
5. ear, early   10. verb, very

Further practice

Teach students one or both of these proverbs:
The early bird catches the worm.
A bird in the hand is worth two in the bush.
Steps:

1. Write "Learn this proverb" and the proverb itself on the blackboard.

2. Discuss the meaning of the proverb at a level appropriate to the students; for example: "People who get up early in the morning are more successful or make more money" for the first proverb.

3. Students learn and practice saying the proverb.

Linking pronunciation with other course work

Tie pronunciation in with practice of:

1. Tag questions using *were/weren't;*

2. Short answers using *were/weren't;*

3. Talking about daily work routine. For example:
   I work in a . . .
   I start work at . . . in the morning.
   I walk/don't walk to work.

Word stress practice

See Overview, pages 11–12.

● • nurses, thirsty, dirty, German, person, circle,
   perfect, colonel, Thursday (and other days of
   the week except Saturday)
• ● prefer, occur

Section B Consonants

The introductory chapter of the Student's Book presents the vocabulary and structures that students will need in order to follow the sound production notes in the units on consonants. The chapter familiarizes students with the parts of the mouth, the types of mouth movements they will use to produce the consonant sounds of English, and the use of the breath (air) and voice in producing consonant sounds.

Work through the chapter with students. It would be helpful for students to use mirrors so that they can watch their own mouths.

UNIT 21 p (pen)

Sound production

See Overview, page 5.

Note: The instructions in the Student's Book describe the production of aspirated p, as it is pronounced before a stressed vowel. Compare the sound *p* has in the words *pie* (aspirated p), *spoon* (unaspirated p), and *cup* (unreleased/unaspirated p).

Variation See notes on the different pronunciations of p under Practice 1 and 2, below.

Student difficulties Arabic and sometimes Vietnamese speakers tend to substitute the sound b for p, for example pronouncing *pie* as *buy*. Speakers of some Asian languages may confuse p and f. Many students, including speakers of Greek, Italian, Spanish, French, Dutch, Japanese, Indian languages, and Slavic languages, may fail to aspirate the sound p at the beginning

of a word or a stressed syllable. Without the puff of air, the sound may be heard as a b by native speakers of English. At the end of words, p is generally not aspirated in English and is often not released (i.e., air is not allowed to escape from the mouth). Students may have difficulty hearing this sound and may omit the p when speaking, or they may pronounce final p too strongly, sometimes adding an extra vowel after it. This may be a particular problem for students who speak languages, such as Spanish, Italian, and many Asian languages, in which words do not commonly end with consonants.

Suggested procedures

Practice 1 and 2 See Overview, page 8.
Note: Each section here practices a different pronunciation of p.

Other words from the dialogue with the sound p: put, pen, pencil, paper, people, past, police officer.

Practice 1 In most of the words here, p is aspirated (accompanied by a puff of air). The sound p is strongly aspirated before a stressed vowel (as in *a pin, Paris, a piece of pie*), less strongly aspirated before l and r (as in *a plastic plate, probably*) or before an unstressed vowel (as in *stupid*). The sound p is not aspirated after s, as in *spoon*.

If students do not aspirate initial p, demonstrate the pronunciation by holding a piece of paper or a lighted match in front of your mouth as you say words like *pen* and *pear*. Have students try this, too; the puff of air should make the paper move or the flame flicker. It may be easier for some students to think of the aspiration as an h sound following the p – as if they were saying pʰie for *pie* or pʰen for *pen*. Respelling words this way on the blackboard may be helpful. To demonstrate the difference between aspirated p at the beginning of a word and unaspirated p after s, hold the paper or lighted match in front of your mouth and say pairs of words like *pie/spy*, *pot/spot*, or *pear/spare*. Students should see the paper or flame move for *pie*, *pot*, and *pear*, and they should see no movement for *spy*, *spot*, and *spare*.

Practice 2   The sound p is very quiet in most of these words. In final position or before another consonant, p may not be released at all, or the release may be inaudible. The mouth forms a p sound, but the lips are kept closed, and the air is not released.

In *stop pulling*, the linked p's are pronounced as one long p, with the first p held and not released until the second p is pronounced.

Note: This description of final unreleased p and linked p's also applies to the other "stop" consonants – b, t, d, k, and g.

Dialogue   See Overview, pages 8–9.

Intonation   Here, students practice intonation in making a list, using short clauses (also see Unit 7). In making a list, each item is usually pronounced as a separate intonation group, with rising intonation on each item except the last, which has falling intonation. Check stress as well as intonation as students practice; both the subject (the person) and the object (the item the person is bringing) should have stress here, since both give new information.

Game   Each student repeats what preceding students said they were bringing and then adds a new item to the list, as in the example. The game ends when the list becomes too long for students to remember it.

Alternative presentation   Introduce the game with students' books closed:
T: We're having a picnic (on Tuesday). I'm bringing (pretzels). (X), what are you bringing?
If X suggests an item that contains the sound p,

indicate that it's OK. If the item does not contain the sound p, it isn't OK. Ask various students what they plan to bring; only items containing the sound p are acceptable. (Instead of using this activity here, it could be adapted to practice or to review a different sound.)

Spelling   Note the double p after short vowels (ɪ, ɛ, æ, ɑ spelled with the letter *o*, and ʌ), as in *happy* or *supper* (compare *paper*, *supermarket*). Call students' attention to the doubling of the p to keep the short vowel sound when endings like -*ing* and -*ed* are added, as in *shopping* or *dropped*; compare, for example, *hopping* and *hoping*.

Many students tend to pronounce all the letters in the written form of a word. They may have difficulty with the idea that some letters are silent, especially if they speak languages in which spelling corresponds closely to pronunciation. Show students that the *p* is silent in words like *psychology*; draw a line through the *p* to show that it is not pronounced.

Further practice

See Unit 22, Further Practice.

Linking pronunciation with other course work

Tie pronunciation in with practice in:

1. Making requests with *please* or *could you help me . . .* ;

2. Expressing wishes with *hope*;

3. Discussing future plans, using *hope to*, *plan to*, *promise to*.

Word stress practice

See Overview, pages 11–12.

●● practice, pocket, present, helpful, Paris, plastic, picnic

• ● surprise, repeat, police, upstairs, perhaps
• ● • spaghetti, potato, impatient, example, official
• ● • • passengers, prob*a*bly, envelope, officer
Note: The word *probably* is sometimes pronounced as two syllables: **prɑbliy**.

UNIT 22 b (baby)

Sound production

See Overview, page 5.

Variation   The sound b is strongly voiced between two vowels, as in *about*. In other positions, it may be partially voiceless.
Note: This note applies to other voiced consonants, too (except for m, n, ŋ, w, y, l, and r).

Student difficulties   Speakers of Arabic may confuse p and b, often replacing p with b, but occasionally doing the reverse and replacing b with p. Spanish and Portuguese speakers tend to pronounce b as a sound that resembles v in some positions (especially in the middle of a word). In some languages, most voiced consonants are pronounced as their voiceless equivalents at the end of words. Students likely to replace voiced b with voiceless p at the end of words include speakers of German, Dutch, Danish, Turkish, Russian, Chinese, West African languages, and sometimes Spanish. Some students may simply drop the final consonant.
   In English, vowels are longer before a voiced consonant than before a voiceless consonant. If students do not lengthen the vowel before a final b, b may be mistaken for voiceless p by English speakers.

Suggested procedures

Practice 1   See Overview, pages 6–7.
   Contrasts for further practice: pill/bill, peas/bees, pat/bat, peach/beach, pack/back, pull/bull, pen/Ben, pole/bowl, pig/big, simple/symbol, cup/cub, rip/rib, mop/mob, lap/lab.

Test   See Overview, pages 7–8. *Answers:*
1. bears   2. path   3. bills   4. cab   5. rope.

Practice 2   See Overview, page 8.
   Other words from the dialogue with the sound b: book, bought, but, been, bedroom, bookshelves, cookbook, paintbrushes.

Dialogue   See Overview, pages 8–9.

Extension   Have a discussion about birthdays, asking questions such as the following:
How do you usually celebrate your birthday? How did you celebrate your birthday as a child?
When is your birthday? (note the form for giving dates: month plus ordinal number)
What do people usually do for birthdays in (student's native country)? (Send cards? Have parties? Have surprise parties? Bake birthday cakes?)
Do you buy people presents for their birthdays? Who do you buy presents for? What was the last birthday present you bought?
What's the best birthday present you've ever gotten?
Have you ever gotten a birthday present you didn't like?

Stress   Here, students practice stress in noun compounds. When two words (both often, but not always, nouns) are used together in English to form a noun compound, the first part of the compound usually has the main stress and the second one has lighter stress. This stress pattern is used whether the nouns are written together as one word (like *bookshelf*) or as two words (like *shopping bag*). Many students have difficulty with this stress pattern, especially as it contrasts with adjective/modifier + noun stress. For example, *a blackbird* (noun compound: **black**bird) is a particular kind of bird, but *a black bird* (adjective + noun: **black bird**) is a bird that is black in color. Similarly, *a greenhouse* is a glass building for growing plants, but *a green house* is a house that is green in color. (See Unit 5 for practice of adjective + noun stress.)
   Note: Not all compounds have first syllable stress. Exceptions include *afternoon*, some adverb compounds (e.g., *however*), and most verb compounds (*understand*, *overlook*, etc.).

Conversation   Students practice in pairs, as in the example, using the following noun compounds: 1. handbag; 2. basketball; 3. ping-pong ball; 4. shopping bag; 5. hairbrush; 6. postcard; 7. cookbook; 8. biology book; 9. paintbrush; 10. birthday card.

Extension   Most names for types of stores are noun compounds. Provide or elicit from students a few examples (e.g., *drugstore, bookstore, department store*). Students then practice as in the following example, using the items from the Conversation:

Example:
A: Where did you get the (handbag)?
B: In a (department store/clothing store).

Spelling   Note the doubling of the letter *b* after short vowels. Make sure students do not pronounce the letter *b* in words like *climb, thumb,* and *doubt.*

Further practice

Joining **p** and **b** sounds between words: When two **p** sounds, two **b** sounds, or a **p** and **b** sound are linked between words, they are pronounced as one long sound, with the first sound held and not released until the second one is pronounced: *to rob banks; stop pushing.*

p + **p** or **b**:
1. Students practice from the blackboard, substituting words beginning with **p** or **b**, using words written on the blackboard, pictures, or real objects as prompts.
I bought some cheap: paper/books/blouses/ pictures/bread/bags/plates, etc.

2. Students practice from the blackboard, using some or all of the following words, choosing the verb *stop* or *keep*:
Stop/Keep: pushing/pulling/breathing/playing/ banging/bragging/practicing/pointing/begging/ barking/painting

Linking pronunciation with other course work

Tie pronunciation in with practice of:

1. Wishing people a happy birthday;
2. Sentences with *but*;
3. Talking about jobs (e.g., asking what someone's job is).

Word stress practice

For further practice of noun compound stress:

1. Contrast noun compound stress with normal adjective + noun stress (both words stressed, with main stress on the noun). For example, have students talk about what people in the class or in a picture are wearing:
  He's/She's/I'm wearing a . . .

  noun compounds: raincoat, rain hat, winter coat, handbag, shoulder bag, sports jacket, T-shirt, etc.

  adjective + noun: blue coat, green jacket, wool coat, leather bag, red bag, striped shirt, long-sleeved shirt, sleeveless dress, etc.

2. Practice noun compound stress in discussing items used on a table or in a kitchen, such as in requesting missing items from a waiter in a restaurant or in buying things for a new house.
Examples:
  tablespoon, teaspoon, steak knife, butter knife, cake fork, water glass, wine glass, soup bowl, soup spoon, serving dish, baking pan, frying pan, teapot, coffee pot, breadbasket, dinner plate, sugar bowl, salt shaker, pepper mill

UNIT 23 t (tie)

Sound production

See Overview, page 5.
  Note: The instructions in the Student's Book

describe the production of aspirated t, as it is pronounced before a stressed vowel. Compare the sound *t* has in the word *tie* (aspirated t) with the sound it has in the word *stop* or *cats* (unaspirated t) and *cat* (unreleased/unaspirated t). Also compare the sound *t* often has in North American English in *city* (flap t).

Variation   See the following sections, Student Difficulties and Practice 1–4.

Student difficulties   Most students do not have difficulty producing a sound approximately like English t, but their exact articulation is likely to differ from a native speaker's. Many students use a dental t (pronounced with the tongue against the top teeth) instead of English alveolar t (with the tongue in back of, and not touching, the teeth). Speakers of Indian languages often substitute a retroflex t (pronounced with the tip of the tongue curled back). Japanese students may pronounce it as tʃ before iy or ɪ and as ts before uw or ʊ. Portuguese students may also substitute tʃ before iy or ɪ.

Many students find the different pronunciations of t in English confusing, especially the flap t sound in the middle of words such as *city*. Some students may not aspirate t at the beginning of a word or syllable, as in *time* or *return*, causing it to sound more like d to native speakers (see notes on aspiration of p, Unit 21, which also apply to t). Students may also have difficulty with t at the end of words, where it is often not released (see Unit 21, and Practice 2 in this unit). An additional pronunciation of t that occurs in North American English is the voiced flap (as in *city* or *little*; see Practice 4). This sound is very confusing for most students, since it is voiced. To some students (e.g., speakers of Spanish or Italian) it may sound more like an r sound in their own languages than a t. Although it is not necessary for students to use the flap t when they speak, it is essential that they recognize this sound as t when they hear it; otherwise they may mistake t for d or r.

Suggested procedures

Practice 1–4   See Overview, page 8.
Note: Each section practices a different pronunciation of t.

Other words from the dialogue with the sound t: take, tall, tennis, tenth, too, to, twelfth, twenty-two, thirteenth, after, downstairs, certainly, exactly, fat, get, short, tight, minutes, store, sheets, want.

Practice 1   In the words in Practice 1, t is aspirated (pronounced with a puff of air). The sound t is strongly aspirated before a stressed vowel (as in *tie*) and less strongly aspirated before an unstressed vowel or before w or r. (See teaching suggestions for aspirated p, Unit 21.) Pairs of words that illustrate the contrast of aspirated t and unaspirated t include: *top/stop, tore/store, tears/stairs, team/steam, tone/stone*. Before r, as in *try*, the position of the tongue for t is a little further back than usual, and the sound often resembles a tʃ sound.
Note: Many people do not pronounce the second t in *twenty*: twɛniy.

Practice 2   The sound t is very quiet (unreleased) in the words in Practice 2. (See notes in Unit 21 on unreleased p, which also apply to t.) The mouth forms a t sound, but the tongue stays on the roof of the mouth and air does not escape. Students may have difficulty hearing this sound and may omit the t when speaking or may pronounce it too strongly.

Practice 3   Many students have difficulty with t in consonant clusters. If necessary, practice buildup of sounds, using cues written on the blackboard. For example:
1. initial consonant clusters
   ssss   ssssstereo   stereo
2. final consonant clusters
   hat   hats
   s   ts   hats

Practice 4   The sound t is pronounced as a voiced flap here. This sound occurs when t comes after a vowel or r and before an unstressed vowel or syllabic l (as in *city*, *party*, and *little*). It also occurs between words, when t is before either a stressed or unstressed vowel (as in *what a* or *get up*). In producing this sound, the tip of the tongue lightly taps the tooth ridge and moves very quickly away (or, before l, does not move away but lets air escape over the side of the tongue to form l). Point out to students that t has a different sound here; tell them it sounds more like a quick English d, and demonstrate its pronunciation. Even if students will not be expected to use this sound when they speak, it is useful to give them some practice saying it in order to familiarize them with the sound.

Dialogue   See Overview, pages 8–9.

Call attention to the "store directory" in the Student's Book to introduce the situation of the dialogue (customers asking for directions in a department store).

Students should look at the directory as they listen to the dialogue. Where more than one possible word is given to complete a sentence, only the first word is said on the Cassette. The other word can be used for additional practice later by the students.

Conversation   Students listen to the dialogue again, following along in their books. Model the examples given in the Student's Book; students listen and repeat. Then, working in pairs, students practice questions and answers from the dialogue. One student asks questions; show students that they can ask for any items presented in the unit (in the practice sections, the store directory, or the dialogue). The other student answers, using the information in the store directory. Students should switch roles.

Spelling   Note the doubling of *t* after short vowels, especially when endings like *-er* and *-ing* are added after a stressed vowel spelled with a single letter plus a final *t* (*hot – hotter, sit – sitting, admit – admitting*). The spelling *tt* also often occurs in the middle of a word after an unstressed vowel when r or a stressed vowel follows, as in *attract, attempt,* and *attack*.

Students often have difficulty with silent letters. Give them practice, according to the level of

the class, in saying the words with silent *t* that they will be expected to know.

Further practice

1. Final **ts**: Practice sentences like these from the blackboard:

There are lots of	pockets	in those	jackets.
	coats		closets.
	students		boats.
	lights		streets.

2. Flap t: Call attention to the flap t when teaching *-er/-est* forms of adjectives (*hotter, shorter, lightest*) or *-ing* or *-ed* forms of verbs (*sitting, writing, waited*).

3. Final t: If students have difficulty with final t, especially if they tend to drop it, have them practice discriminating words that end in unreleased t from words that lack a final consonant. Write words such as the following on the blackboard:

1	*2*
way	wait
tie	tight
star	start
see	seat
pass	past
men	meant
bell	belt
laugh	laughed

Say each pair, reading across; students repeat. Then read words at random from the list; students say whether the word was from Column 1 or 2. Finally, ask individual students to choose words and read them; other students identify which column the word came from.

Linking pronunciation with other course work

Tie pronunciation in with practice of:

1. Asking for and telling the time. Use a teaching clock to practice; for example:

Could you tell me		the time?
		what time it is?
It's	ten	after	twelve.
	twenty	to	ten.

2. Negative short answers. Note that the t in words like *isn't*, *don't*, and *won't* is usually not released.

3. Exclamations: Look at that/What a/Isn't that a . . . (pretty/beautiful/interesting/short/dirty, etc.) (shirt/hat/cat/story/skirt/table, etc.).

Word stress practice

Students listen to the following words and mark the syllable with the main stress by underlining the stressed syllable or by putting an accent mark over the stressed vowel:

1. department   7. teenager
2. typewriter   8. restaurant
3. elevator   9. cafeteria
4. directory   10. salesperson
5. certainly   11. telephone
6. exactly   12. television

Either before or after this, students should practice saying the words. Point out words that have the same stress patterns:

● ∙ ∙ restaurant, certainly, telephone
∙ ● ∙ department, exactly
● ∙ ∙ salesperson, typewriter, teenager
● ∙ ∙ ∙ television, elevator
∙ ● ∙ ∙ directory
∙ ∙ ● ∙ ∙ cafeteria

UNIT 24 d (door)

Sound production

See Overview, page 5.

Variation   The sound d has the same flap sound as t when it occurs after a vowel or r and before another vowel or a syllabic l, as in *Judy*, *harder*, and *pedal* (see Unit 23).

Before r, as in *dry*, the position of the tongue

for d is a little further back than usual, and the sound often resembles a dʒ sound.

Student difficulties   Speakers of German, Dutch, Danish, Russian, Turkish, Thai, and West African languages tend to pronounce d as its voiceless equivalent, t, at the end of words (for example, pronouncing *ride* as *write*). Speakers of Chinese, Portuguese, and Swahili may also confuse t and d. Japanese and Portuguese speakers may pronounce d close to dʒ, especially before the vowels iy and ɪ (for example, pronouncing *deep* as *jeep*). Japanese speakers may pronounce d more like dz before the vowels uw and ʊ (pronouncing *do* as "dzoo"). Spanish and Portuguese speakers tend to pronounce d more like ð in the middle of a word, so that *ladder* may sound like *lather*. At the end of a word, Spanish speakers may pronounce d as a very weak ð or as t, or they may drop the sound entirely. Speakers of Indian languages often substitute a retroflex d (pronounced with the tip of the tongue curled back). Many students use a dental d (pronounced with the tongue against the top teeth) instead of English alveolar d (with the tongue in back of, and not touching, the teeth); although this pronunciation may contribute to a nonnative accent, it does not lead to misunderstandings.

Note that the flap sound (see Variation, above, and Unit 23) may cause some difficulty in understanding, since students occasionally mistake this sound for an r (*jury* instead of *Judy*).

If students confuse t and d, show them that the voice is used for d but not for t. If the d comes after a vowel, make sure that they lengthen the vowel; vowels are longer before voiced consonants in English.

Suggested procedures

Practice 1   See Overview, pages 6–7.
Contrasts for further practice relevant to student difficulties:
t/d two/do, town/down, tear/dare, tear/dear, tie/ die, trip/drip, true/drew, bat/bad, light/lied, neat/need, seat/seed, coat/code, sat/sad, debt/ dead, bet/bed, beat/bead, let/led, hit/hid, built/ build, plant/planned, white/wide

d/dʒ D/G, deep/jeep, dear/jeer, deans/jeans, dim/gym, day/J, dam/jam, Dane/Jane, dust/just, debt/jet, dune/June, do/Jew, paid/page, aid/age, stayed/stage, bad/badge, rained/range

Test   See Overview, pages 7–8. *Answers:*
1. dry   2. time   3. cart   4. writes   5. send.

Practice 2   See Overview, page 8.
Other words from the dialogue with the sound d: day, do, had, played, listened, studied, repaired, cards.

Note:

1. The *d* in *and* is usually not pronounced (ən or n).

2. The name *Judy* is pronounced with the same flap sound as the *t* in *city* (see Unit 23). Many people also use this sound in *nobody, yesterday,* and *today.*

3. Many students have difficulty with the pronunciation of *didn't,* which has a syllabic n (see Unit 41): dɪdnt or sometimes dɪdn.

Dialogue   See Overview, pages 8–9.

Pronunciation   Students practice the three pronunciations of the *-ed* past tense ending, which many students have trouble with, often adding an extra syllable for the *-ed* where they shouldn't or failing to add an extra syllable where it is needed. These pronunciation problems are likely to sound like mistakes in grammar.

Steps:

1. Students listen to and repeat past tense verbs with each of the three pronunciations of the *-ed* ending: d, t, and ɪd.

2. Students listen for the number of syllables in present and past tense forms (add other examples from this list or from the dialogue). They should see that the number of syllables remains the same in the present and past for *rain/rained* and *laugh/laughed* but that an extra syllable is added in *wait/waited* and *need/needed.* On the blackboard, underline the sound/letters before the *-ed* (show that in *laughed* the sound is f). Encourage students to formulate or complete

a rule such as the following: If the (base) verb ends in the sounds *t* or *d,* pronounce the *-ed* ending as an extra syllable. If the verb does not end in these sounds, do not add an extra syllable.

If students add an extra syllable where they shouldn't, draw a line through the *e* in the *-ed,* or respell the word (e.g., *raind*).

3. Write past tense verbs from the first two columns on the blackboard. Underline the sound/letters before the *-ed.* Say the sound. Students repeat, placing their fingers on their throats to see whether or not they use their voices in saying the sound. Help students formulate a rule such as the following: If the (base) verb ends in a sound made with the voice (a voiced sound), the *-ed* ending is pronounced d. If the verb ends in a sound made without the voice (a voiceless sound), the *-ed* ending is pronounced t. (Exception: With verbs ending in t or d, the *-ed* is pronounced as an extra syllable – ɪd.)

4. Add examples of other verbs familiar to students or used in this unit. Either say the past tense form, having students listen and repeat and indicate whether the verb belongs in column 1, 2, or 3; or say the base form (infinitive), having students give the past tense and the column to which it should be added.
Note: The voiceless consonants (other than t) that occur at the end of verbs are p, k, f, s, ʃ, and tʃ. All other consonants at the end of verbs and all vowels are voiced.

Conversation   Students talk about the pictures in pairs, as in the example. Before or after pair practice, check students' pronunciation of the past tense verbs. Ask which sound the *-ed* has in each one. *Note:* Pronunciation of *combed:* kowmd (*b* is silent).

Spelling   *Note:* The spelling *dd* is used in the middle of words after a short vowel sound or before *r, l,* or a stressed vowel. It is also used at the end of words after a short vowel, as in *add* or *odd.*

Introduce or review the spelling rules for the -*ed* past tense:

1. If the verb ends in -*e*, just add *d*: *dance – danced, decide – decided.*

2. If the verb ends in a *y* that follows a consonant, change the *y* to *i* and add -*ed*: *study – studied, try – tried.*

3. If the verb ends in a single consonant after a stressed vowel spelled with a single letter, double the consonant and add -*ed*: *stop – stopped, plan – planned, occur – occurred.* (Exception: The letter *x* is not doubled: *fix – fixed.*)

4. For other verbs, add -*ed*: *rain – rained, play – played, call – called, answer – answered.*

Further practice

1. Some students tend to omit the -*ed* ending when they speak. They may also have difficulty hearing it. Listening practice in discriminating between the present and past tense may be helpful. Read sentences such as the following, choosing one of the verbs (the same sentence can be used more than once). Students indicate whether the sentence was in the present or past tense.

   a. I need/needed money.
   b. You look/looked happy.
   c. They live/lived in France.
   d. I study/studied at the library.
   e. We work/worked all day.

2. Linking of d sounds between words:
On the blackboard, write one column of adjectives ending in d and another of nouns beginning with d. Students use these words to form phrases (have them practice the adjectives first, if necessary). Use the blackboard to show how d sounds are linked; for example, a good dog, an old doctor. The linked d's are pronounced as one long d, with the first d held and not released until the second d is pronounced.

a bad	dog
good	day
hard	dress
cold	desk
wide	doctor
red	door
an old	decision

Linking pronunciation with other course work

Tie pronunciation in with practice of:

1. Simple past tense. For example, tell students to imagine that yesterday they had a bad day. What happened? Why was it a bad day? Provide an example or two, such as:

   Yesterday I had a bad day. I failed a test.
   I missed my train.
   My cat died.

After some practice with this, switch to "a good day."

2. Past perfect tense;

3. *would like/would rather*; for example, pairs of students practice making plans together:

A: What would you like to do tonight/tomorrow/ tomorrow night/Saturday night?
B: I'd like to read a good book/go to bed early/go dancing/listen to the radio/etc. What about you?
A: I'd rather . . .

Word stress practice

See Overview, pages 11–12.
Recognition Test: A ● • B • ● C ● • •
1. forgot [B]   6. damaged [A]
2. today [B]   7. records (noun) [A]
3. children [A] 8. decide [B]
4. repaired [B] 9. radio [C]
5. nobody [C]   10. good-bye [B]

UNIT 25 k (key)

Sound production

See Overview, page 5.

Variation Notes on aspiration of p (see Unit 21) also apply to k. The position of the tongue for k varies depending on what sound comes after it. The tongue is further forward in the mouth when k is followed by a front vowel like iy (as in *key*) and further back when it is followed by a back vowel like uw (as in *cool*).

Student difficulties   Many students, including speakers of Spanish, Portuguese, Greek, Russian, Dutch, and Indian languages, do not aspirate k at the beginning of words. Without the puff of air, k may sound like g to English speakers (for example, making *coat* sound more like *goat*). Aside from this, the sound k is not difficult for most students, although some Arabic students may confuse k and g in all positions, and Turkish speakers may have some difficulty with k before the sounds iy or ɪ.

Suggested procedures

Practice 1 and 2   See Overview, page 8.

Note: Each section practices a different pronunciation of k.

Other words from the dialogue with the sound k: *o'clock*.

Practice 1   In most of the words here, k is aspirated (pronounced with a puff of air). It is strongly aspirated before a stressed vowel (as in *key* or *car*) and less strongly aspirated before a consonant (as in *clock*) or an unstressed vowel (as in *American*). The sound k is not aspirated after s, as in *sky* or *ski*.

See the teaching suggestions for aspiration in the unit on p (Unit 21). Keep in mind, though, that the aspiration for k is likely to be less strong and less dramatically visible (using a piece of paper or a match) than the aspiration for p. The contrast of aspirated k and unaspirated k can be demonstrated with such pairs as *key/ski*, *care/scare*, and *cool/school*.

Practice 2   In the words here, k is usually not aspirated. When k is in final position, as in *look* or *plastic*, it is often not released; the mouth forms a k sound, but no air is let out. Students

may have difficulty with this (see Unit 21 for notes on final unreleased p). Many students, even those who do not otherwise have trouble with it, find the sound k difficult in consonant clusters, as in words like *next*, *excuse*, or *talked*. (Even native English speakers find the cluster skt, as in *asked*, difficult; they often simplify the cluster by leaving out the k sound: æst.) To make words like *talked* or *asked* easier to pronounce, nonnative speakers often pronounce the *-ed* as a separate syllable – a method of simplification that a native speaker would not use. If students do this, write the word on the blackboard and draw a line through the *e* to show that it is not pronounced. At the end of a word like *looked* or *talked* the tongue actually moves very little as it passes from one consonant sound to the next. It may be helpful to tell students to try saying the two sounds – kt – at the same time.

Dialogue   See Overview, pages 8–9.
Check students' understanding of *cuckoo clock*.

Stress   Here students practice stress in noun phrases. The first column uses ordinary adjective + noun stress, in which both adjective and noun are stressed, with the main stress on the noun. The phrases in the second column illustrate adjective + noun compound stress, which combines the adjective + noun pattern with the stress pattern for noun compounds (strong stress on the first element, weaker stress on the second).

Jumbled sentences   Working in pairs, and reversing roles during the activity, students practice sentences with an adjective + noun compound. Go over any unfamiliar vocabulary first.

Spelling   Some of the letters used to spell the sound k are also commonly used for other sounds:
c Before the letters *e*, *i*, and *y*, the letter *c* has the sound s.
ch Usually pronounced tʃ.
x Sometimes *x* is pronounced gz (see Unit 26).

Further practice

1. Final cluster kt: List these or other activities using verbs ending in k + past tense -ed on the blackboard:

    cooked breakfast
    baked a cake
    walked to school/work
    worked/worked for exactly 6 hours
    talked to a cousin/an uncle/a doctor
    looked at pictures/in the mirror
    smoked a cigarette/a pipe/a cigar
    parked a car/a truck

Ask one or two students which of these things they did (specify a time, such as yesterday or during the weekend). Students then practice in pairs, telling each other which things they did. Then ask a few students to report to the class on what their partners did or on the activities that both of them did. (For example: "We both cooked breakfast. We both walked to school.")

2. Final cluster ks: See Unit 26.

3. Linking k sounds between words: See Unit 26.

Linking pronunciation with other course work

Tie pronunciation in with practice in:

1. Telling time using the words *o'clock*, *quarter*, and *six*;

2. Third-person singular of present tense verbs ending with the sound k; for example: likes, looks, makes, asks, speaks, takes, walks, works, drinks, cooks, thinks;

3. Saying "Excuse me," "Thank you," "Thanks," "You're welcome";

4. Order of modifiers in noun phrases.

Stress practice

Recognition Test:
A (adjective/modifier + noun) • •
B (noun compound) • • •

1. a key ring [B]   6. a raincoat [B]
2. a good book [A]   7. a rock band [B]
3. an old coat [A]   8. a gold ring [A]
4. a bank clerk [B] 9. a clean knife [A]
5. a wool skirt [A] 10. a steak knife [B]

UNIT 26 g (girl)

Sound production

See Overview, page 5.

Variation Notes on the position of the tongue for k also apply to g.

Student difficulties At the end of words speakers of German, Danish, Chinese, Russian, Turkish, and some West African languages may pronounce g as k, its voiceless equivalent (for example, pronouncing *dug* as *duck*). Vietnamese and Thai speakers may have difficulty with g at the beginning of a word; Thai speakers may replace it with k, and Vietnamese speakers may use a more guttural sound. Some speakers of Arabic may have difficulty with g and substitute either k or dʒ. Some speakers of Japanese may pronounce g as ŋ between vowels. Dutch speakers tend to replace g with the sounds k or x (the non-English sound in *Bach*). Greek and Spanish speakers may use a softer (non-English) sound rather than the hard stop sound g in some words. Some students, including speakers of Spanish and Chinese, have difficulty in general with consonants at the ends of words and may either drop a final g or pronounce it as a voiceless k. Many students do not lengthen the vowel before final voiced consonants like g, leading to possible confusion between words ending in voiceless k and voiced g.

For students who substitute k for g, show that the voice is used for g.

Suggested procedures

Practice 1 See Overview, pages 6–7.
  Note: Some people pronounce the word *clog*

with the vowel ɔ instead of ɑ; for these people *clock* and *clog* are not a sound contrast pair.

Contrasts for further practice: coast/ghost, could/good, cot/got, came/game, cave/gave, clue/glue, crab/grab, crow/grow, card/guard, come/gum, picky/piggy, rack/rag, Dick/dig, pick/pig, peck/peg, buck/bug, duck/dug, lock/log (for some people, not a sound contrast pair).

Test See Overview, pages 7–8. *Answers:*
1. goat 2. bag 3. classes 4. clocks 5. curl.

Practice 2 See Overview, page 8.
Other words from the dialogue with the sound g: go, got, gave, game, Gloria.
Note: At the end of a word, as in *dog*, stop sounds like g are often unreleased (see Unit 21, on p).

Dialogue See Overview, pages 8–9.
Note: There is no g sound in words like *coming, sing,* or *songs*. The *ng* spelling in these words has the sound ŋ. Pronunciation of *England:* ɪŋglənd.

Stress See the discussion of stress in Unit 16.
Make sure students understand the principle of writing telegrams – that you use only the most important words in writing them, the words necessary to communicate the information, since you have to pay for each word. Usually, this means using just content words (nouns, verbs, adjectives, adverbs) and leaving out "grammatical" words (like prepositions, articles, conjunctions, and pronouns). Just as these content words are the most important in conveying a message in a telegram, they are the most important in communicating when we speak, and are therefore the words that are stressed. Similarly, the words that can be omitted from a telegram because they are not essential for conveying the message are usually words that are not stressed in speech.
To help with stress, the teacher and/or students should clap or tap the rhythm while saying the sentences. You may also want to demonstrate by saying the longer sentence at the same time that a student says the shorter, "telegraphic" sentence. The longer sentences will probably take a little longer to say than the tele-

graphic sentences, but they should not take *much* longer to say, since the number of stressed syllables is the same.

Extension If students have difficulty with, for example, lines from a dialogue, use the telegram idea to work on the rhythm. Students pretend they are writing a telegram and change the sentence into the form it would have in a telegram. They then practice saying first the telegraphic form of the sentence and then the full sentence.

Spelling Note that words ending in the letters *ng* do not have the sound g.

Further practice

Even students who do not have difficulty with the sounds k and g alone may have problems with them in certain environments:

1. Final clusters ks and gz: Students practice "X likes..." substituting words such as dogs/eggs/clocks/lakes/rugs/frogs/snakes/cakes/long walks, using blackboard prompts or pictures as cues. For X, substitute the name of an imaginary person, a famous person, or someone in the class.

2. Linking k and g between words: When two stops like k and g link two words, the sound is held briefly and then released: *a big garden; a sick cat*. Practice the following (or part of it) from the blackboard. Then have students practice in pairs, taking turns asking and answering questions, and later reporting the answers.

k k Do you like: cooking/cold coffee/cleaning/cats/kittens/carrots/caves/quiet places/quiet people/cards/kites/cake?

k g Do you like: games/golf/gardening/getting presents/giving presents/going to parties/guns/gray hair/grapes?

g g Do you like big: gardens/glasses/gold rings/green snakes?

g k Do you like big: classes/crowds/coats/kitchens/cups?

Linking pronunciation with other course work

Tie pronunciation in with practice of:

1. Requests beginning "Could you give me..." or "Could you get me...";

2. *Go + -ing* verb; for example, "Let's go jogging/dancing/shopping/etc. together" or "Would you like to go jogging/swimming/etc.?"

Word stress practice

See Overview, pages 11–12.
Recognition Test: A • •   B • •   C • • •   D • • •
1. again [B]   6. England [A]
2. guitar [B]   7. Chicago [D]
3. forget [B]   8. telegram [C]
4. together [D]   9. beginning [D]
5. August [A]   10. arriving [D]

Point out that in words in which the first syllable is *a-, be-, ex-, for-, re-,* or *to-,* this syllable is likely to be unstressed: again, about, arrive, begin, below, example, exam, exactly, excuse, expensive, forget, repeat, remember, tomorrow, together.

UNIT 27 s (sun)

Sound production

See Overview, page 5.

Student difficulties   Most students can pronounce the sound **s**. Speakers of Greek, Italian, and Spanish may replace it with **z** before **m** or other voiced consonants (e.g., "zmall" for *small*); Germans may substitute **z** before a vowel ("zo" for *so*). Some students confuse **s** and **ʃ** (see Unit 29); speakers of European Spanish and Portuguese, for example, may pronounce **s** so that it sounds like **ʃ** in some words. Japanese speakers may replace **s** with **ʃ** before **iy** and **ɪ** (e.g., *she* for *see*).

Many students have considerable difficulty with consonant clusters containing **s**. Students likely to have such problems include speakers of Spanish, Portuguese, Chinese, Japanese, Arabic, Turkish, Farsi, some Indian languages, Thai, Vietnamese, Swahili, and many other Asian and African languages. When an *s + consonant* cluster occurs at the beginning of a word, students most commonly insert a vowel either before the cluster or after the **s**, resulting, for example, in pronunciations like **ɛspuwn, ɪspuwn,** or **sɪpuwn** for *spoon*. Less frequently, students (e.g., speakers of Vietnamese and some other Asian languages) may drop the **s**, saying **puwn** for *spoon*. German students, following the sound and spelling patterns of their own language, may pronounce **s** as **ʃ** in initial consonant clusters, so that *spoon* sounds like **ʃpuwn**. Clusters with three consonants (as in *spring* or *straight*) are especially difficult for students.

In the middle of a word, students often drop one of the consonants in a cluster, saying "esplain" for *explain*. Words with more than one cluster may cause particular problems.

In final clusters, students may insert a vowel or, more commonly, drop one of the consonants (usually the last one), saying "des" for *desk* or "tes" for *test*. In final clusters of *consonant + s,* as in plural endings (e.g., *cats*), many students drop the final **s**, though some may insert a vowel either after the cluster or between the consonants, saying **kætsə** or **kætɪs** for *cats*. Even students who do not normally have difficulty with consonant clusters (e.g., Russian speakers) are likely to have problems if one of the consonants is **θ**, as in *sixth* or *months*. Consonant clusters with more than two consonants are also a particular problem. Students may either insert vowels or drop consonants, for example, saying "ness" for *next*. Clusters across word boundaries are also likely to present problems; students may add extra vowels in phrases like *this street* or *next stop*.

For students who have difficulty with **s** + *consonant* clusters, it may be helpful to have them lengthen the **s**. For example:

ssss   sssstay   stay
jusssss   jusssst   just

In a word like *speak*, tell students to lengthen the **s** and then close their lips for **p** while still saying **s**.

If students add a vowel before initial clusters, it may also be helpful to contrast words that begin with a cluster and words that begin with a vowel + a cluster: *state/estate, sleep/asleep, spot/a spot.*

In words with final consonant clusters, forward and backward buildup may be helpful:

let   let's;   s   ts   let's

In words spelled with *x*, showing students a simplified transcription may help them know what pronunciation they should be aiming at; for example: ekspensiv (*expensive*) or nekst (*next*).

Note that native English speakers also find certain consonant clusters difficult and sometimes simplify them by dropping a consonant, as in æst for *asked*, fɪfs for *fifths*, and tɛksbʊk for *textbook*.

Suggested procedures

Practice 1 and 2   See Overview, page 8.

Other words from the dialogue with the sound s: so, sun, yes.

Dialogue   See Overview, pages 8–9.

Joining sounds   Students listen and repeat after the Cassette or the teacher. Many students have difficulty linking s sounds smoothly between words. They may add extra vowels, especially where there are consonant clusters.

Linked s's between words are pronounced as one long sound. If students have difficulty, practice some examples from the blackboard:

letssssit

letsssstay

Note that the t in *just* may be dropped when another consonant follows: "jussit."

Further practice from the dialogue: six star.

Drill   Students practice consonant clusters with final s in plural nouns and present tense verbs. Some sentences have linking s's as well as final clusters: *wants some, collects stamps.* Students listen and repeat the example. Then the teacher (or a student) reads the sentences in the book, choosing sentences in random order, and stu-

dents supply the answers, as in the example. Use backward buildup or blackboard practice with linking s if necessary (see above). If the next word begins with a vowel, the final consonant cluster can be simplified by dividing it between the words: *laugh sat.* If students do not make the consonant before the s (in final *consonant* + s clusters) quiet enough, the following blackboard practice may be helpful:

CAt   CAtS

BOOk   BOOkS

STAMp STAMpS

Conversation   Model the example, either by yourself or with a student. Then have students practice in pairs. Make sure they realize that B chooses only one response.

Intonation in alternative questions with *or*: rising intonation before the word *or*; falling intonation at the end (see Unit 1).

Reading   Students listen to the reading played on the Cassette or as it is read aloud by the teacher. Then students practice reading aloud, with particular attention to s + *consonant* clusters. Mark linking s's if students have difficulty. Make sure students do not substitute the sound z in words like *smile* and *smoke*.

Spelling   The fact that the sound s has so many spellings may be confusing to students. Point out that most of the spellings contain the letter *s* or the letter *c* (followed by *e*, *i*, or *y*). Note that the letter *s*, especially between two vowels, is also a common spelling for the sound z (see Unit 28).

Go over the pronunciation of some of the words with silent consonants; in words listed for the spellings *ps*, *st*, and *sw* (under Other Spellings), the *p*, *t*, and *w* are silent.

If students make mistakes in pronouncing the letter *c*, a quick review may be helpful. Write words such as the following on the blackboard or flash cards, and have students say whether the *c* in each one has the sound s or k:

exercise accountant

recent   innocent

decorate cycle

recipe

Linking pronunciation with other course work

Tie pronunciation in with practice of:

1. Suggestions beginning *Let's*;

2. The simple present tense of verbs having the sound s in the third-person singular; for example: asks, breaks, cooks, counts, drinks, drops, eats, forgets, gets, keeps, likes, looks, makes, puts, shuts, sits, sleeps, speaks, stops, takes, waits, walks, wants, works, writes.

Word stress practice

See Overview, pages 11–12.
- • hotel, collect, instead, across, upstairs, outside (*Note:* In the last two words, the first syllable has a light stress.)
- • • special, silly, slowly, basket, silver, stolen, slippers, carrots, Sunday, seashore, headaches, suitcase (*Note:* In the last three words, the second syllable has a light stress.)
- • • • sensible, stupidly, possible, interesting, bicycle, Saturday
- • • • expensive, exciting, potato

UNIT 28 z (zoo)

Sound production

See Overview, page 5.

Student difficulties   Many students have difficulty with the sound z, including speakers of Spanish, Italian, Portuguese, Chinese, Vietnamese, Thai, Turkish, German, Dutch, and West African, Scandinavian, and Indian languages. The most common error is to replace this sound with s, especially at the end of a word, so that *eyes* sounds like *ice*. (Many students also pronounce the vowel before a final z as too short, causing confusion with s.) Spanish, Chinese, Thai, and Scandinavian speakers tend

to have difficulty with z in all positions in words. Japanese speakers may replace z with dz or, before the vowels iy and ɪ, with dʒ, pronouncing *zoo* as "dzoo" or *zip* as "gyp." Speakers of some Indian and other Asian languages may also confuse z and dʒ.

If students confuse s and z, practice of the sound in isolation is helpful. Point out that the voice is used when making the sound z but not when making the sound s. Demonstrate by placing your hand on your throat and moving it to show the vibration as you say z. Students should be able to feel the vibration with their hands placed over their ears or on their throats as they say z. Note that voicing may not be as strong when z occurs in a word, especially at the beginning or end.

Many students have difficulty with z in final consonant clusters. Their most common errors are to omit the final z or to add a vowel between the preceding consonant and z; a vowel sound is particularly likely to be added if there is a vowel letter in the spelling, as in *loves*. Clusters ending in z occur mainly when the ending -(e)s or 's is added to form a plural, possessive, contraction, or a third-person singular present tense verb. Use backward buildup (see Unit 27 on s) to practice these clusters. Respelling the word with a final z instead of an s is also helpful: dogz.

Suggested procedures

Practice 1   See Overview, pages 6–7.
   Note: Pronunciation of the letter *z*: American ziy; British zɛd. In contrasting s and z at the end of words, make sure students make the vowel longer before z.
   Contrasts for further practice: sink/zinc, lacy/lazy, racer/razor, race/raise, ice/eyes, peace/peas, niece/knees, place/plays, loose/lose, since/sins.

Test   See Overview, pages 7–8. *Answers:* 1. Z   2. buzz   3. sip   4. raise   5. price.

Practice 2   See Overview, page 8.
   Other words from the dialogue with the sound z: Valdez (often pronounced with a final z sound in English, s in Spanish).

Dialogue See Overview, pages 8–9.

Note: *Ugh* can be pronounced in various ways: ʌ, ʊ, or with final consonant sound g or x (as in *Bach*), etc.

The dialogue provides extensive practice of the sound s, as well as the sound z. Make sure students clearly distinguish between the two sounds. (Words with s: post office, this, say, six, mice, it's, sack, snakes, strange, hissing, sound, listen, what's, box.)

Pronunciation Many students have difficulty with final *-s* endings. They not only have the problem of remembering to add the sound s or z but also have the difficulty in many words of pronouncing a final consonant cluster with these sounds. Particularly if students drop the final s or z sound, pronunciation difficulties will sound like grammar mistakes, whether or not they actually are.

Steps:

1. Students listen to and repeat words with each of the three pronunciations of the *-s* ending: s, z, and ɪz. The words in the upper half are plural nouns; below are third-person singular present tense verbs (the verbs are not on the Cassette).

2. Students practice saying words from the first two columns. Underline the letter/sound before the *-s* ending in a few words; have students say it. Ask students whether or not each sound is made using the voice; ask the same question about the sounds "s" and "z" that head each column. Students should see that after a voiceless sound (p, t, k, f, θ) the *-s* ending is pronounced s; after a voiced sound (b, d, g, v, ð, m, n, ŋ, l, r, and all vowels), it has the sound z.

Note: If students add an extra syllable where the ending is spelled *-es* in the first two columns, draw a line through the *e* to show that it is not pronounced, or respell the word omitting the *e*.

3. For words in the third column, write the singular form for the nouns or the base (infinitive) form of the verbs. Underline the final letter/sound. (Point out that the letter *x* in *box* is pronounced ks.) Students say the words and then the final sound alone. With students' help, make a list of the sounds (s, z, ʃ, ʒ, tʃ, dʒ) that

are followed by *-es* pronounced as an extra syllable ɪz. These are all sibilant ("hissing") sounds or sounds that contain a sibilant (like tʃ). Note that the plural and third-person singular endings are always spelled *-es* after these sounds, not just with s.

4. Add examples of other words used in the unit or otherwise familiar to students. Give the singular form of the noun or the base form of the verb; students pronounce the word with *-(e)s* added and say which column it belongs in.

Conversation Students look at the chart and make sentences, as in the example. This can be done in groups or by the whole class. If necessary, tell students that "so do" has the same meaning as "do, too": "Liz wears glasses and so do I" is the same as "Liz wears glasses and I do, too." (If necessary, also show the connection of *do* to the first part of the sentence – "I wear glasses, too.")

Joining sounds The sound z at the end of a word becomes s when the next word begins with s, as in the following example:
Whose is it? huwz ɪz ɪt
Whose seat is it? huw(s)siyt ɪz ɪt
This happens frequently, especially with such common structure words as *these, those, is, whose, who's,* and *his.*

Further practice:

1. Practice the present progressive in the third-person singular, using sentences that describe students or pictures. Linking s will occur when the verb begins with s; for example: "He's sleeping." "She's swimming." "Who's smiling?" "Maria's studying English."

2. Students all change seats at random. Then choose two students and have them practice the following dialogue:
A: Whose seat are you in?
B: Y's seat.
A: Who's sitting in your seat?
B: Z's sitting in my seat.
(Note the contrast of the vowels ɪ and iy here.)

Spelling Spellings for the sound z that use the letter *s* may cause difficulty, especially because there is no foolproof way to predict which sound (s or z) the letter *s* has in an unfamiliar word. Note, though, that when the letter *s* falls between voiced sounds (e.g., between two vowels) or between a vowel and a final *e*, it more regularly represents the sound z than the sound s. In other cases (e.g., when it is an initial *s*, or doubled, or next to a voiceless sound), the letter *s* is more likely to represent the sound s. Note that the *s* spelling in the words *use* and *close* can represent either the sound s or z, depending on the part of speech the word acts as.

Many students pronounce the *s* spelling in words like *present*, *cousin*, and *noise* with the sound s even if they can say the sound z; extra practice with such words is helpful for them. For review, give students a list of words containing the letter *s*; students say whether *s* has the sound s or the sound z in each word. For example:

1. busy
2. worse
3. surprise
4. present
5. sensible
6. opposite
7. sense
8. cousin
9. has
10. lose

board. Write words such as those listed under the headings on flash cards. Have students read the word aloud and say which group it belongs to.

Families
mothers, fathers, brothers, sisters, uncles, babies, boys, girls, grandfathers, grandmothers
Bodies
fingers, hands, arms, heads, eyes, ears, legs, toes
Animals
dogs, horses, donkeys, llamas, lions, tigers, leopards, zebras, bears, wolves, camels, monkeys, pigs, cows
Schools
teachers, pupils, lessons, questions, answers, examples, words, numbers, letters, pictures, pens, pencils
Times
hours, days, years, mornings, afternoons, evenings
Rooms
chairs, tables, beds, walls, floors, ceilings, corners

Further practice

1. If students tend to drop the final *-s* in their speech, they may also have difficulty hearing it. They may find it particularly difficult to hear the extra ɪz syllable after a sibilant sound. Give students practice in listening for the *-s* ending. Use pairs of words such as the following. Read one word from each pair and have students indicate which of the words they hear.

noise – noises
teach – teaches
package – packages
wash – washes
bus – buses
box – boxes
office – offices
lose – loses
dish – dishes
language – languages
watch – watches
surprise – surprises

2. Final z in plurals:
List headings such as the following on the black-

Linking pronunciation with other course work

Tie pronunciation in with practice of:

1. Introductions: "This is Mr./Mrs./Ms. X";

2. The simple present tense of verbs having the sound z in the third-person singular.

Word stress practice

See Overview, pages 11–12.
Recognition Test: A ● ●   B ● ●   C ● ● ●
1. surprising [C]
2. because [B]
3. always [A]
4. office [A]
5. contains [B]
6. present (noun) [A]

7. surprises [C]   9. amazing [C]
8. surprise [B]   10. package [A]

UNIT 29 ʃ (shoe)

Sound production

See Overview, page 5.

Student difficulties   The sounds s and ʃ are confused by speakers of Greek and by some speakers of Dutch, European Spanish, Indian languages, and Swahili (see also Unit 27, Student Difficulties). Chinese speakers may have difficulty with the sound ʃ, too, confusing it with s or pronouncing it in a way that sounds foreign to native English speakers. Japanese and Chinese speakers may confuse ʃ and h before the vowels iy or ɪ, so that they do not clearly distinguish words like *he* and *she*. Speakers of Thai, Vietnamese, and especially Spanish may substitute tʃ for ʃ.

For students who find ʃ difficult, spend some time on the mouth position and practice of the sound in isolation. Tell students who confuse s and ʃ to round their lips and slowly move their tongues back as they make the sound s. It may help for them to exaggerate rounding their lips at first. For those who replace ʃ with tʃ, demonstrate that the sound ʃ can be sustained and that tʃ cannot. Also point out that for tʃ the tip of the tongue touches the roof of the mouth (for the t part of the sound) while for ʃ it does not.

Suggested procedures

Practice 1   See Overview, pages 6–7.
Contrasts for further practice relevant to student difficulties:
s/ʃ seat/sheet, sign/shine, sew/show, sort/short, suit/shoot, said/shed, same/shame, self/shelf, sock/shock, fasten/fashion, iris/Irish, class/clash, mass/mash, Russ/rush
h/ʃ he/she, heat/sheet, hip/ship, he'd/she'd, he's/she's, heel (*or* he'll)/she'll, heap/sheep

Test   See Overview, pages 7–8. *Answers:*
1. Sue's 2. sheets 3. sign 4. leash 5. shell.

Practice 2   See Overview, page 8.
Other words from the dialogue with the sound ʃ: should, shrunk.

Dialogue   See Overview, pages 8–9.
Have students listen to the dialogue with their books closed. Tell them they are going to listen to a conversation between a man and a woman that takes place in a store. Write a few questions such as the following on the blackboard, to be answered by the students after they listen to the dialogue:
What is the woman shopping for?
What does the man do? (his job)
Does the woman buy anything? Why?/Why not?
Note: Students who tend to confuse s and ʃ may have difficulty pronouncing *Sid, Sally, see, sell,* and *sale.* Check to make sure they do not substitute ʃ in these words.

Joining sounds   Students listen and repeat. Two ʃ sounds, or a s and a ʃ sound (as in *Swiss chalets*), are linked and pronounced as a single ʃ sound. (This also often occurs when a final z sound is followed by ʃ: *is she* ɪʃiy.)
Note the stress on both words: **Span**ish **shoes,** **Eng**lish **sheep,** etc.

Conversation   Students practice the conversation, as in the model. This may be done in pairs, with students switching roles, or in a larger group as a chain drill.

Word stress   Endings added to words in English often cause changes in the way the word is pronounced, especially in the placement of stress. The strong stress often shifts to a different syllable. Here students practice the stress pattern of words ending in -ion and the shift in stress that often occurs when this suffix is added to a verb. The strong stress moves to the syllable before the *-ion*. The words practiced here also have a second, lighter stress on the first syllable.

Spelling   The variety of spellings (other than *sh*) for the sound ʃ may cause confusion. Point out that many of the other spellings tend to occur in certain endings (e.g., *-ion, -ial,* and *-ious*). In other places, these spellings (e.g., *ti, ci*) are pronounced as an ordinary consonant + vowel. Some of the other spellings (e.g., *ce, ch*) occur only rarely with the sound ʃ.

Further practice

Practice names of nationalities with the sound ʃ: Swedish, Danish, Turkish, Polish, Spanish, Finnish, Irish, Scottish, English, British, Russian. For example:

1. Ask questions about the nationality of students or of people (especially women) known to the class. For example:
TEACHER: Is X Swedish or Danish?
STUDENT(s): She isn't Swedish *or* Danish! She's Polish.
TEACHER: Is Y from Turkey?
STUDENT(s): Yes. She's Turkish.
Or use similar questions, but with reference to languages spoken rather than to nationality.

2. Do a chain drill. The teacher or a student begins by saying, "I think she's (Danish)." The next student says, "Are you sure? I think she's (Polish)." Students continue, using as many nationalities with the sound ʃ as they can think of or practicing from a list on the blackboard.

3. Using students' suggestions, make a list of famous people of the nationalities mentioned above. Then practice questions and answers: "What nationality is X?" "He's/She's . . ."
    Examples: Margaret Thatcher (English); James Joyce (Irish); Sir Walter Scott, James Watt (Scottish); Alfred Nobel (Swedish); Hans Christian Anderson (Danish); Miguel de Cervantes, Hernán Cortés (Spanish); Kemal Ataturk (Turkish); Mikhail Gorbachev, V. Lenin, Leo Tolstoy (Russian); Jean Sibelius (Finnish).

Linking pronunciation with other course work

Tie pronunciation in with practice of:

1. *should/shouldn't*: Have students read statements, choosing either *should* or *shouldn't* according to their opinion; for example, "Capital punishment should/shouldn't be legal."
2. Talking about nationality.

Word stress practice

Note that the nouns *conversation* and *information* also have verbs related to them: *converse* and *inform*. When the ending *-ation* is added, it causes a change in the pronunciation of the vowels in these words as well as a shift in the stress. For further practice, give students other verbs that follow the patterns presented; students form the corresponding noun (e.g., *graduate, concentrate, celebrate, illustrate, continue, reserve, administer*).

UNIT 30 ʒ (television)

Sound production

See Overview, page 5.
    Note: The sound ʒ rarely occurs at the beginning of words in English. It occurs initially only in words borrowed from other languages, especially from French (for example, *genre*).

Student difficulties   Many students find the sound ʒ difficult, including speakers of Greek, Italian, German, Dutch, Scandinavian languages, Japanese, Thai, Indian languages, Chinese, and sometimes Arabic. Many Spanish speakers also have difficulty with this sound, although some South Americans do not, since it occurs in words spelled with *ll* in some dialects. Students tend to replace the sound ʒ with sounds close to dʒ, ʃ, or z, or sometimes with zy, under the influence of the spelling (e.g., in *measure*).

Sound contrast pairs with ʒ and other sounds are extremely rare and tend to include rather obscure words (e.g., *legion/lesion, pledger/pleasure, Caesar/seizure*).

Students can practice ʒ by using nonsense words that contrast ʒ and the sound with which it is confused (for example, *zoo/zhoo, wash/wazh*), following the procedures for sound contrast pairs used elsewhere in the book. If students substitute dʒ, point out that ʒ can be sustained and dʒ cannot; if they substitute ʃ, focus on the voicing of ʒ. If students confuse ʒ with z, it may be helpful to exaggerate the rounding of the lips for ʒ.

Suggested procedures

Practice 1   See Overview, page 8.

Reading   Students listen to the television schedule on the Cassette or read by the teacher, repeating after each line or at the end of the schedule. Note that the reading also gives practice in the other sibilant sounds taught: s (six, seven, special, across, science, it's), z (news, clothes, Shakespeare's, Martians), ʃ (fashion, special, show, fiction, Shakespeare's, Martians).

Conversation   Students practice questions and answers as in the example, working in small groups. Check stress. After the first time the question is asked, *you* will have stress: "What are **you** going to watch on television tonight?"

Note: going to is often pronounced gənə.

Drill   Students practice the response "It was my pleasure" or "My pleasure." Practice the sentences with students, checking the rhythm and stress. Make sure students do not stress words like *for* and *me*; students also sometimes put too much stress on *you* in "Thank you." Tap or clap to show the rhythm, or write sentences on the blackboard (for example, "THANK you for FIXing my TELevision"). (Grammar: Note the use of the *-ing* form of the verb after the preposition *for*, if this is new for students.)

Note: (for more advanced students) When the

sound z at the end of a word is followed by the sound y at the beginning of the next word, the two sounds are often combined in informal speech to form ʒ, as in *use your* in sentence 4 (yuwz + yər – yuwʒər). This often happens with forms of the word *you* (as in How's/Where's/Is/Here's your . . . ").

Word building   Students listen to and repeat pairs of words: a verb and a related noun form ending in *-ion*. In these pairs, the final d sound in the verb changes to ʒ in the noun that ends in *-ion*. Call attention to this by underlining the *d* (or *de*) in the verb and asking students what sound this has. Then underline the *si* (or just the *s*) in the noun and ask students what sound that has. Note that in the last three pairs, the vowel sound also changes from ay to ɪ (*divide* dɪvayd, *division* dɪvɪʒən).

Other pairs for further practice:

conclude – conclusion	persuade – persuasion
confuse – confusion	revise – revision
include – inclusion	supervise – supervision
exclude – exclusion	provide – provision
delude – delusion	erode – erosion

Practice 2   Working alone or in pairs, students fill in the blanks with an *-ion* noun formed from the underlined verb. (Answers: decision, explosion, collision.) Answers can be written on the blackboard by a student or checked by students in pairs.

Spelling   The spellings for the sound ʒ may cause difficulty for students, since they are all regular spellings for other, more common sounds. Note that the letter *s* has the sound ʒ only before the letters *i* or *u*.

Linking pronunciation with other course work

Tie pronunciation in with practice of:

1. The reply "It's a pleasure" or "My pleasure";

2. Descriptions of daily routine using the word *usually*; for example, use pictures or other

prompts to practice questions and answers such as, "What time do you usually get up/have breakfast/leave the house/get to work/have lunch/get home/eat dinner/go to bed?" "I usually get up at . . ."

Word stress practice

- •• special, local, treasure, measure, leisure, island, program, fashion, science
- •• tonight, across, report, decide, garage, police, collide, invade, explode, resign
- ••• casual, leisurely, measuring, treasury
- ••• occasion, invasion, explosion, collided, decision, decided
- •••• secretary, television
- •••• variety, unusual

Point out classes of words that follow similar stress patterns:

1. Words that end in *-ion* (main stress on the syllable before the *-ion*): occasion, collision, invasion, explosion, decision, division, fashion, fiction, conversation; *exception*: television;

2. Words that end in *-ual* or *-ial* (stress usually on the syllable before the ending): casual, unusual, special, usually;

3. Words with unstressed prefixes *a-, de-, re-, to-, in-, ex-*: across, decide, report, resign, tonight, invade, explode.

UNIT 31 tʃ (chair)

Sound production

See Overview, page 5.

Student difficulties   French, Portuguese, Dutch, Greek, Scandinavian, and some Vietnamese speakers have difficulty with the sound tʃ. Such students commonly replace it with ʃ. Greek students may also replace it with ts, and Scandinavians may pronounce it as ty. Chinese speakers may use a foreign-sounding pronunciation of the sound. Some students, including speakers of Thai, Lao, and Khmer, may have some difficulty with the sound at the end of words, often replacing it with t. Italians do not have trouble with tʃ, but may make mistakes because of spelling, pronouncing the spelling *c* or *cc* before *e* or *i* (as in *accent* or *city*) as tʃ or pronouncing the spelling *ch* as k. Spanish speakers do not have difficulty with tʃ, but need practice in learning to discriminate tʃ from ʃ, since they often substitute the former for the latter.

Suggested procedures

Practice 1   See Overview, pages 6–7.
   Contrasts for further practice: shows/chose, share/chair, sheet/cheat, sherry/cherry, she's/cheese, shin/chin, shore/chore, mash/match, dish/ditch, crush/crutch, marsh/march, wish/witch (or which).

Test   See Overview, pages 7–8. *Answers:*
1. chop   2. ships   3. sheep   4. wash   5. chose.

Practice 2   See Overview, page 8.
   Other words from the dialogue with the sound tʃ: cheaper.

Dialogue   See Overview, pages 8–9.
   Note: For more advanced students, you may want to point out that the sound tʃ often occurs in informal speech when the sounds t and y are linked between words, as in *get you* gɛtʃə ("What can I get you today?").

Recipe   Students listen to the recipe on the Cassette or as it is read by the teacher, looking at the pictures in their books. Then they listen again, this time repeating. Note the use of "list" intonation (practiced in Units 7 and 21) in naming the ingredients at the beginning of the recipe and in steps 2 and 3.
   Possible activity for additional practice: Write each step of the recipe on a strip of paper (prepare more than one set for larger classes). Mix up the strips so that the steps are not in order, and give each student one of the strips. Books should be closed. Each student reads aloud the step written on the piece of paper. Students then

try to arrange their steps in the order of the recipe. They should do this without looking at one another's slips, which may have to be read aloud several times. If students decide on an order different from the one in the book, it should be accepted as long as it makes sense.

Conversation In groups, students plan an imaginary meal. Before they get into groups, write on the blackboard a list of foods that have the sounds ʃ and tʃ, using students' suggestions. (The English names of many foods have these sounds. Some examples, in addition to those given in the recipe, include chicken, chocolate, chestnuts, french fries, cherries, chick-peas, anchovies, artichokes, chives, peaches, fish, shrimp, mashed potatoes, squash, sugar, and pistachio nuts.)

Extension Students dictate a recipe for a dish in their imaginary dinner. Tie this activity in with practice in listing steps in a sequence, using words like *first*, *then*, and *next*.

Spelling Practice tʃ in words that contain the sound spelled with the letter *t*, a spelling that students may find confusing. After practicing the words shown in the Student's Book, write a few more examples on the blackboard (e.g., *furniture, agriculture, manufacture, culture, statue*); students try pronouncing them. Review the *t* spelling as used for different sounds. Give students a list of words. They say which sound *t* has in each word: t, ʃ (as in *shoe*), or tʃ (*chair*). For example:

1. picture
2. question
3. conversation
4. practice
5. century
6. return
7. initial
8. vacation
9. natural
10. future

Further practice

1. Using the foods shown for the recipe or foods from the meals planned in the Conversation, students pretend they are in a store asking for prices; for example: "How much are the chops?/ How much is a can of chicken broth?/How much

do the mushrooms cost?" The teacher or another student should give answers to the questions.

2. Joining sounds: See Unit 32.

Linking pronunciation with other course work

Tie pronunciation in with practice of:

1. Count and noncount nouns and describing quantities using *how much* and *too much*;
2. Questions with *which*;
3. Structures using *such* or *such a*.

Word stress practice

See Overview, pages 11–12.
Recognition Test: A ● ●   B ● ●

1. chicken [A]
2. mushrooms [A]
3. machine [B]
4. salad [A]
5. mixture [A]
6. powder [A]
7. shampoo [B]
8. of course [B]
9. include [B]
10. chili [A]

Review stress in noun compounds:

lamb chops   **chili** pepper
butcher shop   **chili** powder
shoulder chops   **wash**ing machine
chicken broth

Compare: a de**li**cious **chick**en (adjective + noun)

UNIT 32 d3 (joke)

Sound production

See Overview, page 5.
Use the instructions in the Student's Book. Or tell students to first practice d and 3. Tell them to begin to make d. Then they should slowly move their tongues away from the roofs of their mouths as they say 3.

Student difficulties Many students have difficulty with the sound d3. Portuguese, French,

Vietnamese, and sometimes Dutch speakers may pronounce it as ʒ, Greeks as ʃ or dz, Danes and Norwegians as dy, Swedes as y, and Thais as tʃ. Spanish speakers may confuse dʒ and y or may substitute tʃ for dʒ. German, Dutch, and Turkish speakers often substitute tʃ for dʒ, especially at the ends of words. Some Arabic speakers may also have difficulty. Some students, for example, Germans and Scandinavians, substitute y for dʒ, a problem that may be reinforced by the spelling: The letter j, which in English usually represents dʒ, represents the sound y in some other languages (as in the German, Dutch, Norwegian, Danish, and Swedish word *ja*, meaning "yes").

In teaching, emphasize that the first part of this sound is a d.

Suggested procedures

Practice 1   See Overview, pages 6–7.
Contrasts for further practice relevant to student difficulties: tʃ/dʒ: cherry/Jerry, chain/Jane, choice/Joyce, chin/gin, etch/edge, batch/badge, rich/ridge, larch/large.
It may also be helpful to contrast the sounds d and dʒ (see Unit 24).
ʒ/dʒ: See Unit 30, under Student Difficulties.
Use nonsense words to contrast sounds like dy and dʒ if students confuse them.

Test   See Overview, pages 7–8. *Answers:*
1. choking   2. Jerry's   3. jeered   4. ages
5. matches.

Practice 2   See Overview, page 8.
Other words from the dialogue with the sound dʒ: John, dangerously, larger.

Dialogue   See Overview, pages 8–9.
Note: For more advanced students, you may want to point out that the sound dʒ often occurs in informal speech when the sounds d and y are linked between words, as in *did you* dɪdʒə ("Did you hear how it happened?").
With students who tend to substitute dʒ for y, check pronunciation of the word *yes*.

Joining sounds   Unlike many other consonants, the sounds tʃ and dʒ are not linked and pronounced as one long sound when they come together between words. Both sounds are pronounced separately.

Extension   For additional practice in joining the sounds tʃ and dʒ, have students practice a conversation like the following:
A: How much *(cheese) did you get/eat/buy?
B: (any answer that makes sense, e.g., "a pound," "a small piece")
*Students substitute words such as the following, using prompts from the blackboard, cue cards, or pictures: cheese, jam, chocolate, juice, chicken, Jello, jelly, cheesecake, chocolate cake, cherry pie, Japanese food, Chinese food, chili.

Crossword puzzle   Students can do the crossword puzzle in class, working in pairs, or at home, checking their answers during the next class with another student. All of the answers have the sound tʃ or dʒ.
Answers:
Across: 1. Churchill   4. jam   5. jar   6. choc-(olate)   7. chose   8. por(ch)   10. such
Down: 1. chicken   2. reach   3. larger   4. Jock's   5. jeep   9. (j)ok(e)

Spelling   The letter *g* before *e, i,* or *y* usually has the sound dʒ. Exceptions include *get, forget, give, begin,* and *together*. For review, give students a list of words spelled with *g*, such as those in the list below. Have students circle the letters that have the sound g and underline the letters that have the sound dʒ. Examples: ⓖood; large.
1. again   6. manager
2. German   7. begin
3. original   8. dangerous
4. guest   9. village
5. dialogue   10. forget

Further practice

1. Using the illustrations in the book, each student asks a question about the page it is on. For example:

s: Which page has a picture of a (zoo)?
t: Page 30.
s: No. Page 90.
The number of pages could be limited, for example, to Units 1 through 10.

2. Tell students the following anecdote (once): "A new shopping center has three butcher shops next to each other. The name of each butcher is Joe. When the three butcher shops open, the first butcher writes above his shop, 'Joe's – the Largest Butcher Shop.' The second butcher writes above his shop, 'Joe's – the Cheapest Butcher Shop.' The third butcher writes above his shop in large letters, 'Joe's Butcher Shop – Main Entrance.'"

Ask students to say all the words they remember. Write the words on the blackboard as they say them. As a review, you may want to group words by sound in columns, asking students which column to add each word to:

s center, shops, next, first, writes, largest, second, cheapest, entrance

z has, is, his, Joe's, letters

ʃ shopping, shops, shop

tʃ butcher, each, cheapest

dʒ Joe, Joe's, largest, large

Read the anecdote again. Have students add words they missed the first time. Ask for a volunteer to retell the anecdote, or ask students to work in pairs or small groups and try to write out the complete story. Then ask for volunteers to tell it. Finally, provide students with the original version.

Linking pronunciation with other course work

Tie pronunciation in with practice of structures using *just*.

Word stress practice

● ● • dangerous, manager, passenger, agency, difficult, orange juice

● ● • rich children, large cherries, teach German, change classes, prime minister

UNIT 33 f (fan)

Sound production

See Overview, page 5.

Student difficulties   Although most students do not have problems with the sound f, it may be difficult for speakers of Indian languages, Tagalog, and some Asian languages (though not Chinese). The sound is usually confused with the sound p. Japanese students often confuse it with h, especially before vowels made in the back of the mouth like uw or ɔ.

Suggested procedures

Practice 1 and 2   See Overview, pages 6–7.
   Contrasts for further practice relevant to student difficulties:
p/f put/foot, pill/fill, past/fast, pin/fin, pine/fine, pat/fat, pull/full, pool/fool, pour/four, pork/fork, paint/faint, pair/fair, pile/file, prize/fries, supper/suffer, cheap/chief, leap/leaf
h/f hold/fold, hey/Fay, honey/funny, her/fur, hire/fire, hair/fair, hear/fear, he/fee, hue/few, height/fight, hit/fit, home/foam, horse/force, halt/fault, who'll/fool, who'd/food

Test   See Overview, pages 7–8. *Answers:*
1. peel   2. hold   3. cuff   4. pan   5. fall
6. Hey!

Practice 3   See Overview, page 8.
   Note: Call attention to the shift in stress between **pho**tograph and pho**tog**rapher.
   Check the pronunciation of the consonant cluster f + r (as in *front, friendly*).
   Point out that *of* has the sound v, not f, unless

it is linked to a following f sound, as in *of February*.

Other words from the dialogue with the sound f: *fine, fill out, sofa, if*

Dialogue   See Overview, pages 8–9.

Check students' understanding of vocabulary that may be unfamiliar, either before or after they listen to the dialogue. For example, use photographs or blackboard sketches to check their understanding of *profile/front*. Ask students to find another word in the dialogue that has a meaning similar to *cheerful* (*happy*).

Intonation   When a clause with *if* begins a sentence, it often has a slight rise: If Fred laughs, he looks funny. This is not the only intonation possible, however. The *if* clause could also, for example, end with a slight rise and fall: If Fred laughs, he looks funny. Note that in both cases the sentence is said with two intonation groups rather than as a single phrase. Students should follow the model provided on the Cassette or by the teacher. Use gestures or arrows drawn on the blackboard to show the direction of the intonation.

Jumbled sentences   Working in pairs or groups, students find the clause in the second column that best finishes the sentence begun in the first column. Students should take turns reading the sentences.

Spelling   *Note:*

1. In a few words, the combinations *lf* and *ft* have the sound f (*l* and *t* are silent): *half, calf, often, soften*;

2. The pronunciation of the vowels in words spelled with *augh* or *ough* is likely to cause confusion:

   æ laugh
   ʌ enough, rough, tough
   ɔ cough

The spelling *ough* may also be pronounced as ɔ (*thought, bought*, etc.), ow (*though*), uw (*through*), or ɑw (*bough*). The spelling *augh* is usually pronounced ɔ (*caught, taught*, etc.). In all of these words, the *gh* is silent (it does not make an f sound).

Practice the stress in words ending with *-graphy* and *-grapher*: • ● • • photography, photographer, geography, biography

Further practice

Students read the following groups of words from the blackboard and say which word doesn't belong in each group, and why:
1. wife knife father grandfather   [knife]
2. fifty four first fifteen   [first]
3. fly fish fruit beef   [fly]
4. football foot finger face   [football]
5. left fought fell forget   [forget: present tense]
6. funny fat friend careful   [friend: noun]

Linking pronunciation with other course work

Tie pronunciation in with practice of:

1. Conditional sentences using *if*. For example, students can practice a chain drill in which one student begins by making a conditional sentence starting with *if*. The following student makes another *if* sentence based on the first one, and so on. For example (unreal conditional):
A: If I were rich, I wouldn't work.
B: If I didn't work, I'd travel a lot.
C: If I traveled a lot . . . etc.

2. The words *before, after* (*that*), *first*, and *finally* when used in describing a sequence of events or explaining the steps involved in doing something.

Word stress practice

See Overview, pages 11–12.
A. Recognition Test: A ● •   B • ●   C ● • •
1. prefer [B]   6. frightened [A]
2. myself [B]   7. forget [B]
3. cheerful [A]   8. difficult [C]
4. different [A]   9. finished [A]
5. comfortable [C]   10. sofa [A]

B. The words below have more than one stress. In addition to the main stress, they have a lighter, secondary stress. Tap or clap to demonstrate the rhythm. Students listen and repeat.
● ● ● photograph, telephone
● ● ● grandfather
● ● ● ● operator, February
● ● ● ● information

UNIT 34 v (van)

Sound production

See Overview, page 5.

Student difficulties   The sound v is difficult for speakers of Arabic, Chinese, Japanese, Hindi, Punjabi and other Indian languages, Korean, Spanish, Thai, Lao, and Khmer. Dutch, German, and Turkish speakers may also have difficulty with the sound, especially at the end of words, where v is likely to be replaced by f, so that *leave* is pronounced like *leaf*. Other students, such as speakers of Arabic, tend to substitute f for v in all positions; Chinese speakers may also substitute w. Japanese and Spanish speakers often replace v with b, pronouncing *very* as *berry*. Spanish speakers may pronounce both the letters *b* and *v* as a b sound at the beginning of a word, but as a sound closer to v (but made with the two lips, rather than the lips and teeth) between vowels. Many students, including speakers of German, Indian languages, Russian, Scandinavian languages, Thai, Farsi, and Turkish, confuse v and w, most often replacing w with v, but sometimes replacing v with w or producing a sound somewhere between the two.

For students who confuse v and f, practice with the sound in isolation is helpful, emphasizing the use of voice in v but not in f; students can place their fingers on their throats to feel the voicing. They should feel their lower lips vibrate when they pronounce v but not when they pronounce f. Also note that a lot of air is produced when saying f, but not when saying v. For students who confuse b and v, contrast the lip posi-

tions using physical demonstrations and/or blackboard sketches. Tell students to press their two lips together to produce b, but to "bite" the lower lip with their teeth to produce v. Also show that the sound b cannot be prolonged, whereas v can be. For students who confuse v and w, contrasting the lip positions is helpful; see Unit 35.

Suggested procedures

Practice 1 and 2   See Overview, pages 6–7.

Note: The *l* is silent in *half, halves, calf, calves.*
Contrasts for further practice relevant to student difficulties:
f/v feel/veal, fail/veil, fee/ V, fast/vast, fault/vault, fat/vat, ferry/very, refuse/reviews, safe/save, life/ live (adjective) (also see pairs under Related Words Ending in f and v)
b/v berry/very, bet/vet, bat/vat, bolts/volts, curb/ curve, bent/vent, bow/vow, bowel/vowel, marble/marvel, cupboard/covered

Test   See Overview, pages 7–8. *Answers:*
1. vest   2. boat   3. few   4. fan   5. halve
6. calves.

Practice 3   See Overview, page 8.

Dialogue   See Overview, pages 8–9.

Extension   Students ask and answer questions like the ones in the dialogue, for example:
How long have you lived here?
Have you lived here for a long time?
Has your family lived here for very long?
When did you move here?
Do you have a nice view from your house?
Do you like living here?
Provide a model and/or blackboard prompts for the questions, such as, "How long/lived here?" "When/move here?" This practice may be expanded into short dialogues developed by students working in pairs.

Reading   Have students read the paragraph silently first. When they have finished, ask one or two volunteers to read it aloud, choosing the words in parentheses that describe the picture. Then ask one or more students to describe the picture, looking just at the picture and not at the paragraph.

Related words ending in f and v   Students listen to the pairs of words on the Cassette or read by the teacher and then practice saying them. For example, to practice the singular and plural forms of nouns, the teacher says either the singular or plural form and a student responds with the other form. Make sure students pronounce the *-es* plural ending as the sound z (no extra syllable): leaves liyvz.

Note that the letter *v* is always followed by the ending *-es*, never by *-s* alone.

Other words that follow the same patterns:
Singular – Plural: half – halves, self – selves, loaf – loaves, thief – thieves, shelf – shelves, wolf – wolves
Noun – Verb: relief – relieve, grief – grieve

Add some of these for further practice, choosing words students are likely to know.

Note: Not all nouns ending in f form the plural this way; exceptions include roof – roofs and belief – beliefs.

Spelling   The sound v is written with the letter *v* (except in the word *of*). Note that the letter *v* is not doubled, even after short vowels, as in *river*, *never*, *having*, and *giving* (compare *dinner*, *better*, *happen*, *sitting*, etc.). Point out to students that when the sound v comes at the end of a word, the letter *e* is always added in the spelling, even in words with short vowels (as in *give*, *have*, and *love*).

The word *have* may be pronounced with the sound f when it is followed by a voiceless consonant, as in *have to*.

Further practice

If students confuse the sounds b and v, dictate jumbled spellings of words with the letters *b* or *v*. For example:
RYVE [very]

ABBY   [baby]
BULE   [blue]
VEMO   [move]
ISTIV   [visit]
Students unscramble the words. To check the answers, they dictate the words or the spellings of the words to a student who writes the answers on the blackboard.

Linking pronunciation with other course work

Tie pronunciation in with practice of:

1. Present perfect:
a. "How long have you lived/been here?" "Have you lived here for a long time?" "How long have you been studying English?" etc.;
b. Asking and talking about past experience, using "Have you ever...?" "No, I've never.../ Yes, I have/No, I haven't."

2. *very:* for example, in contrasting *very* and *too;*

3. *should have/shouldn't have/could have/couldn't have/would have*, and so on (pronunciation of *have* – əv).

Word stress and syllable practice

A ● (one syllable) moved, lived, leaves, knives, loves, gives, lives, view
B ● • valley, village, farmer, visit, never, forest, lovely, driving, evening, every, *family
C • ● • November, arriving, fantastic
*Some people pronounce this as three syllables.

Read words at random from the above lists. Students indicate whether the word belongs to group A [●], B [● •], or C [• ● •]. Students should practice saying the words either before or after doing this. Make sure that they do not drop the final d or z sound in words like *moved* or *loves* or add an extra syllable in these words or in *evening* or *every*.

UNIT 35 w (window)

Sound production

See Overview, page 5.

w is a glide sound. It is close to the English sound uw. Have students first practice uw. Tell them to make their lips round and hard for w. The sound w is a short sound. The lips move quickly into position for the next sound.

Variation   Some people pronounce the *wh* in *what, where, when,* and most other words spelled with *wh* as the sound hw (exceptions include *whole, who,* and words derived from *who,* such as *whose,* where the *wh* is pronounced as h). Many other people pronounce the *wh* spelling as w. It is probably best for students to follow their teacher's pronunciation model. This book does not show the sound hw. (Even among speakers who distinguish between the sounds w and hw, the use of w in place of hw is very unlikely to cause misunderstandings.)

Student difficulties   Speakers of many languages, including German, Dutch, Slavic languages, Hebrew, Hungarian, Turkish, Farsi, Scandinavian languages, Indian languages, Japanese, Spanish, Portuguese, and Greek, tend to have difficulty with this sound. Many of these speakers (e.g., speakers of German, Scandinavian and Slavic languages, Turkish, and sometimes Italian) replace w with v (pronouncing *west* as *vest*), but they may also sometimes replace v with w (pronouncing *vest* as *west*). Dutch, Lao, and Farsi speakers also confuse w and v or make an intermediate sound for both. Spanish and Greek speakers may replace w with gw, g, or a similar sound, saying *good* for *wood* or *would.* Some students may confuse w with r or use a sound resembling b. Speakers of Spanish, Japanese, and some other Asian languages have particular difficulty in pronouncing w when it is followed by ʊ or uw, as in *woman.*

For many students, seeing the correct lip position through both physical demonstration and a diagram is helpful. It may also help them to

practice saying uw smoothly before vowels (e.g., you – uw – all – wall; you – uw – ill – will). Students who replace w with v should be careful not to let their bottom lip touch their upper teeth at all. Even speakers who do not have trouble with this sound in isolation may have difficulty saying it in clusters such as tw, kw, sw, or skw (as in *twenty, quiet, sweater,* or *squirrel*).

Suggested procedures

Practice 1   See Overview, pages 6–7.

Contrasts for further practice relevant to student difficulties:

v/w verse/worse, vine/wine, vent/went

b/w ball/wall, B (*or* be)/we, bell/well, bill/will, bird/word, best/west, bent/went, buy/Y (*or* why), bet/wet, big/wig, bake/wake, bear/wear, born/worn

g/w good/wood (*or* would), gun/won (*or* one), guest/west, gate/wait, gave/wave, get/wet, guide/wide

hw/w which/witch, why/Y, where/wear, whether/weather, wheel/we'll, whale/wail, whine/wine

Test   See Overview, pages 7–8. *Answers:*
1. we   2. vest   3. whales   4. worse   5. veal.

Practice 2   See Overview, page 8.

Other words from the dialogue with the sound w: with, was, walked, away, highway.

Note: Some people say the *wh* spelling in words like *what, when,* and *everywhere* as the sound hw.

Dialogue   See Overview, pages 8–9.

If students confuse the sounds v and w, check their pronunciation of words with v: *Vera, Victor, very, veal,* and so on.

Intonation   Students practice falling tone intonation in statements and wh-questions asking for information. For both types of sentences, the voice usually rises on the last stressed syllable and then falls.

Extension   Write some (or all) of the wh-words (*who, what, when, where, why,* and *how*) on the blackboard. Ask students for more examples of wh-questions (and answers), either about the dialogue or about each other. If students have difficulty with the stress or intonation, write the sentence on the board using capital letters for the stressed syllables (with larger capitals for the main stress), making the words curve up or down according to the intonation: who WENT for a W A L K

Jumbled answers   Students practice in pairs. One student asks a question from the first column; the other student finds the correct answer in the second column. Students can take turns asking the questions.

Spelling   Students may find the spellings of the sound **w** with a vowel letter (*u* or *o*) confusing. Note that the *u* in *qu* regularly represents the sound *w*, but that the *u* in *gu* and *su* has the sound **w** only in a few words. In most words with *gu*, the *u* is either silent (as in *guest*) or is pronounced as a vowel sound (as in *gum*); in *su*, the *u* usually has a vowel sound (as in *sun, sure,* etc.).

Further practice

Students choose the correct word to begin the following questions about the picture in Unit 34: *Which* or *What?*
_____ person is waving? (The farmer.) [Which]
_____ kind of car is the farmer driving? (A van.) [What]
_____ time of year is it? (Fall.) [What]
_____ is the weather like? (Sunny./Fine.) [What]
_____ plant is losing its leaves? (The vine.) [Which]

Linking pronunciation with other course work

Tie pronunciation in with practice in:

1. Talking about the weather: "What's the

weather like in . . . ?" Explain that "What's the weather like?" means "How is the weather?" Discuss what the weather is like at different times of year and/or in different places. In a class of mixed nationalities, discuss the students' own countries. In a class consisting of students of one nationality, discuss different towns or regions known to them.

It's	(very)	warm.
It's not		wet.
		windy.

2. Asking questions using *why, what, where, when, which;*

3. Telling time. Using a clock with movable hands or a clock drawn on the blackboard, have students practice asking for and giving the time. For example:

A: What time is it?/Do you know what time it is?

B: It's	a quarter	after	twelve.
	twenty	to	one.
			five.
			seven.
			eleven.

4. Questions with *will* or *would,* used, for example, in offering things: "Would you like a/some . . . ?" "What would you like to drink?"

5. Identifying individual things or people, using *which one;* for example:
   a. identifying items when shopping: "Which one do you want?" "This one/that one/the one with the . . . ";
   b. identifying people in a photograph: "Which one is your mother?" "The one with the red sweater."

Word stress practice

Read the following pairs of words. Have students say whether the stress patterns were the same or different. Students should practice saying the words before or after doing this.
1. highway,   2. sandwiches,
   away [D]   wonderful [S]

3. Wednesday, 5. o'clock, twenty [D]
   window [S] 6. anyway, everywhere [S]
4. sweaters,   7. everyone, November [D]
   windy [S]

UNIT 36 y (yellow)

Sound production

See Overview, page 5.

Student difficulties   The sound y is pronounced as dʒ, or a sound close to dʒ, by many
Spanish speakers. Some German speakers may
also confuse dʒ and y. Some Portuguese speakers may tend to omit the sound y. Chinese and
Japanese speakers may find it difficult before the
sounds iy or ɪ, as in *year*.

Show students that the tongue position for this
sound is initially more or less the same as for the
sounds iy or ɪ. Unlike the position for dʒ, the tip
of the tongue should not touch the roof of the
mouth. Begin with practice of some words with
iy or ɪ, for example *eat, easy, is*. Then practice a
few words beginning with y, using the blackboard to show the similarity of y to iy or ɪ. Write
a word like *you* or *yes*, erase the letter *y*, and replace it with EE or II: EEou (or IIou), EEes (or
IIes). y is a glide sound; in producing a glide, the
mouth is not in a fixed position. The tongue
glides smoothly as it moves from y into the
vowel that follows.

Suggested procedures

Practice 1   See Overview, pages 6–7.
Contrasts for further practice: jet/yet, Jello/yel-
low, Jack/yak, jell/yell, jewel/you'll, juice/use
(noun).

Test   See Overview, pages 7–8. *Answers:*
1. Yale 2. jam 3. yolk 4. years 5. Jess.

Practice 2   See Overview, page 8.

Other words from the dialogue with the
sound y:
New York, Yoko
student, new: Some people (e.g., British speakers) pronounce these words with the sound y:
styuwdnt, nyuw.
Pronunciation of *use*: noun yuws; verb yuwz,
but *used to* yuwstə.
Note: If students substitute the sound y for dʒ,
check their pronunciation of *Jack, jacket*, and *jazz*.
Make sure, for example, that they do not use the
same sound for *Jack* and *Yoko*.

Dialogue   See Overview, pages 8–9.
Explain any unfamiliar vocabulary – for example, *peculiar* (odd, strange), *millionaire* (a person who has a million dollars; a very rich person) – before students listen to the dialogue.
Note: For more advanced students, you may
want to point out that when the sounds d and y
are linked between words, they are often pronounced as dʒ in informal speech: *did you* dɪdʒə.

Pronunciation   *Used to* and *use to* both have
the same pronunciation: here, yuwstə. (At the
end of a sentence, the final sound can be a full
vowel instead of ə.)
Students listen and repeat after the Cassette or the
teacher. If necessary, check students' understanding of *used to* to describe past states or habits by asking questions; for example, "Did you use to live in
[student's hometown]?" "Where did X use to live?"
"Does X live there now?" Students should understand that "He used to play the piano" means that
he played the piano in the past but probably does
not play the piano now.

Conversation   Students practice asking and
answering questions in pairs, as in the example.
When a clause with a word like *when* (or *before,
after, if*, etc.) begins a sentence, it is usually pronounced as a separate intonation group ending
with a slight fall or rise:
When you were younger, did you use to play the
piano?
When you were younger, did you use to play the
piano?
Have students practice this before they begin.

Use gestures or arrows on the blackboard to show the intonation.

Extension   Ask other questions with *used to*. For example:
What did you use to be afraid of (as a child)?
What did you use to do that you don't do now?

Spelling   The sound y as part of the spelling *u* causes difficulty for many students, who often find it hard to know when to use a y sound and when not to. The Student's Book gives the basic rules for when to say the sound y. It might be best to go over the rules one at a time, checking students' understanding by asking them to try pronouncing some additional words, ones with and without the y sound. You may also want to discuss some of the following notes on the rules shown in the Student's Book:

1. The sound y does not occur if the letter *u* is followed by two consonants (*upper, umbrella, butter, husband,* etc.) or by a single final consonant (*us, but*).

2. *Rule 2:* (a) The consonants listed (p, b, m, etc.) are all sounds made without using the front of the tongue; (b) the sound y does not occur if the *u* is after a *g* and followed by a vowel (*guess, guide*).

3. *Rule 3:* The y sound also occurs, but more rarely, with other consonant sounds: r (*erudite*), d (*pendulum*), θ (*Matthew*), and for some speakers s (*peninsula*).

Possible words for students to try pronouncing: upset, ugly, unite, unkind, uniform, uneasy, mute, acute, husband, ruler, amusing, puppy, fuel, humid, glue, assume, manufacture.

Note: British speakers and some Americans use rules slightly different from those given in the Student's Book. These speakers use the sound y in more places, for example, after the consonants t, d, n, and sometimes s, z, l, and θ (such as in *news* nyuwz).

Further practice: relaxed speech

In relaxed conversation, the sounds d and y may be linked between words to form dʒ. This hap-

pens especially when the second word is a form of the word *you:* did you dɪdʒə. Although students do not need to use this pronunciation in their own speech, they should be aware of it so that they can better understand native English speakers.

Write on the blackboard:

dʒ‿
did you

Compare *do you:*   do you

There is a contrast between the sounds dʒ and y in *did you/do you*. (In very rapid speech, the phrases may be reduced to *did you* dʒə vs. *do you* dyə.)

Write the following sentences on the blackboard or on a paper handout. Read the sentences at a rapid, conversational speed; have students listen and fill in the blanks for each of the following sentences, writing either *do you* or *did you*. In *do you, you* has the sound y. In *did you*, students should hear the sound dʒ.

1. Where ___ ___ live?   [Where do you live?]
2. When ___ ___ come here?   [When did you come here?]
3. ___ ___ see that car?   [Did you see that car?]
4. ___ ___ like it?   [Do you like it?]
5. How ___ ___ feel?   [How did you feel?]
6. What ___ ___ want to do?   [What do you want to do?]

Linking pronunciation with other course work

Tie pronunciation in with practice of:

1. Affirmative short answers beginning with *yes;*

2. Talking about the past using *used to;*

3. Talking about being or becoming accustomed to things, using *be used to* or *get used to;*

4. Sentences with *usually,* used, for example, in talking about past activities or present routines;

5. Interviewing someone by asking questions

beginning "Do you/Are you/Have you/Can you," etc. For example, one student goes to the front of the room and pretends to be a famous person. The other students ask yes/no questions (e.g., "Are you American?" "Do you live in Hollywood?") to try to figure out who the famous person is. Put a limit (such as 20) on the number of questions that can be asked.

Word stress practice

See Overview, pages 11–12.
Recognition Test: A ● ● ●   B ● ● ●   C ● ● ●
1. computer [B]   6. opinion [B]
2. musician [B]   7. company [A]
3. familiar [B]   8. peculiar [B]
4. curious [A]   9. any more [C]
5. millionaire [C] (or [A]) 10. interview [A]

UNIT 37 h (hat)

Sound production

See Overview, page 5.
   Note: The position of the tongue and lips for h depends on the sound that follows.

Student difficulties   The sound h occurs very frequently in such common words as *he, her, his, have, how, who,* and so on. It is very difficult for some students to pronounce.

Group 1   Speakers of French, Portuguese, Italian, Hebrew, and some African languages, as well as some speakers of Turkish, tend to omit the sound h and/or overcompensate by adding it unnecessarily in front of words beginning with a vowel. Students tend to put h in the wrong place more frequently as they get more worried or self-conscious about not saying this sound when they should. Encourage those who omit h to connect words smoothly in phrases, without stopping their breath. Emphasize the fact that a lot of air is needed to produce this sound.

Group 2   Speakers of Greek, Spanish, Slavic languages, Arabic, and Chinese tend to pronounce h as a harsh sound, like the non-English sound x in *Bach.* For these students:
a. Emphasize the fact that the tongue is not used in producing this sound. Practicing h first before vowels made with the tongue low in the mouth will help students keep the back of the tongue down. Tell them to keep the tongue down as they say *hot, happy,* and *how.*
b. Show that the sound is like panting hard after running.
c. Show that a lot of air is needed to make this sound. Hold a strip of paper in front of your mouth and make the sounds x and h to show the difference in effect.

Group 3   Japanese speakers tend to confuse the sound h with f when it occurs before back vowels like uw, but they confuse it with ʃ before iy or ɪ. Chinese speakers also confuse the sounds s, ʃ, and h when they occur before the sounds iy or ɪ. This confusion is particularly noticeable in the words *he* and *she.* Calling students' attention to the difference in mouth positions may be helpful. For h before iy or ɪ, the tongue is arched, and the tip of the tongue touches the lower teeth. For ʃ (see Unit 29), the front of the tongue is grooved, and the tip does not touch the lower teeth. The lips for h are slightly spread; for ʃ they are slightly rounded.

Suggested procedures

Practice 1   See Overview, pages 6–7.
The contrast practiced here is helpful for both Group 1 and Group 2 students who have difficulty with the sound h.
   Contrasts for further practice relevant to student difficulties:
no sound/h I/high, air/hair, ate/hate, all/hall, and/hand, ear/hear, ow!/how, at/hat, Ed/head, it/hit, I'd/hide, eel/heel
ʃ/h she/he, she's/he's, sheet/heat, sheep/heap, sheer/hear, ship/hip, she'll/heel

Test   See Overview, pages 7–8. *Answers:*
1. heat   2. high   3. air   4. hate   5. art.

Note: Pairs of sentences with this sound contrast (no sound vs. h) are rare, so omission of the sound h seldom causes misunderstanding in meaning at the sentence level.

Practice 2   See Overview, page 8.

Other words from the dialogue with the sound h: how, Henry, have/had, he, his.

Dialogue   See Overview, pages 8–9.
Note:

1. With students who tend to insert h's unnecessarily in words beginning with a vowel, check the pronunciation of words and phrases like *hello Ellen, how awful, a horrible accident, express, operation,* and *ambulance.*

2. The sound h is often dropped in unstressed words like *he, her, have,* and *his* in connected speech (but not at the beginning of a sentence). Point out places where this is likely to happen, for example, "on *his* way home from work," "Was *he* hurt?," "behind *his* house."

3. Use the dialogue to practice questions with *how, who, who's,* and *whose.* For example, have students choose the correct word to begin questions like these:

_____ had an accident?
_____ did it happen?
_____ husband had an accident?
_____ in the hospital?

Intonation   Students practice intonation in exclamations, which often have a wider intonation range than ordinary statements. The last stressed syllable is said at a higher pitch than usual and is followed by a sharply falling tone. Exclamations expressing surprise and dismay, like the ones practiced here, are also often said rather slowly, with the stressed vowels prolonged.

The intonation of many foreign students may tend to sound flat to native English speakers. To encourage students to use a wider voice range here, write examples on the blackboard like this:

Model the intonation. Use hand gestures or draw arrows to demonstrate the intonation or to correct problems.

Conversation   Students listen to the example read by the teacher and repeat or follow along in their books. They then practice the conversation in pairs, substituting names from Column 1 in the first blank, sentences from Column 2 in the second blank, and exclamations in Column 3 in the third blank.

Note: In relaxed speech, native English speakers would be likely to omit the sound h in the words *his* and *herself* as they are used in the sentences.

Reading   Students fill in the blanks in the anecdote with words from the list, either in class or as homework. After students check their answers (e.g., in pairs), they should listen to the anecdote read by the teacher and then practice reading it aloud.

Spelling   The sound h is usually spelled with the letter *h.* Note that the letter *h* also occurs in the combinations *sh, ch, th,* and *ph,* where it does not have the sound h. In a few words, sequences like *th* and *ph* belong to different word parts (e.g., *hot + house*) and the letters are pronounced separately. The spelling *wh* is usually pronounced as the sound w (or hw; see Unit 35); in *whole, who,* words derived from *who,* and a few other words, the *wh* spelling has the sound h.

The silent letter *h* is difficult for many students, who may be confused about when to pronounce h and when not to. Go over the pronunciation of words in which *h* is silent. Point out, for example, that the word *hour* is pronounced like *our.* For later review, give students a list of words such as the one below. Ask them which words have the sound h (make sure they focus on sounds, not spellings).

1. hour   6. how
2. hear   7. who
3. whole   8. hole
4. unhappy   9. phone
5. why*   10. honest

*The answer could vary, depending on whether speakers say *wh* here with the sound w or hw.

Further practice: relaxed speech

Many students have difficulty distinguishing unstressed pronouns in rapid conversation, especially when the *h* is dropped and the vowel is reduced in pronouns like *he, him, his,* and *her*. Give students practice in listening for reduced pronouns. For example, write a sentence frame like "Give ___ the book." on the blackboard. Tell students to listen and fill in the blank with the word they hear. Read the sentence several times, varying the pronoun that you say. Make sure to read the sentence rapidly, using reduced forms.
1. Give him the book.
2. Give her the book.
3. Give her the book.
   etc.
Then change sentences; for example, "I saw ___ brother."
1. I saw her brother.
2. I saw your brother.
3. I saw his brother.
4. I saw our brother.
   etc.

Linking pronunciation with other course work

Tie pronunciation in with practice of:

1. Questions beginning with *whose* and answers with possessive pronouns *his/hers*. For example, using pictures, objects, or words on the blackboard as prompts, students practice questions and answers:
[*prompt*] handbag
A: Whose handbag is this?
B: It's hers.
As prompts, try to include words beginning with h or with sounds likely to be confused with h, words such as *handbag, hat, photo, food, apple, house, earring, horse, hand, hairbrush,* and *handkerchief*.

2. Questions beginning with *how, who, how much, how many, how often;*

3. The greetings "Hello," "Hi," "How are you?" and so on;

4. Exclamations beginning with *how;*

5. Structures with *have/has* and *his/her/hers* (make sure the words are not in a position where the h would be dropped).

Word stress practice

See Overview, pages 11–12.
Recognition Tests:
A ●• B •●
1. hello [B]   6. hammer [A]
2. behind [B]   7. herself [B]
3. husband [A]   8. afraid [B]
4. awful [A]   9. happened [A]
5. express [B]   10. all right [B]
A ●•• B •●•
1. ambulance [A]   6. unhappy [B]
2. hospital [A]   7. important [B]
3. horrible [A]   8. accident [A]
4. imagine [B]   9. opinion [B]
5. terrible [A]   10. remember [B]

UNIT 38 θ (think)

Sound production

See Overview, page 5.

Student difficulties Nearly all students, except speakers of Greek and Castilian Spanish, have great difficulty with the sound θ, replacing it with s, t, f, or sometimes ʃ. Students find the sound particularly difficult to pronounce in final consonant clusters, as in *fifth, sixth,* or *months*. (See the note under Linking Pronunciation with Other Course Work in this unit.)

Showing students the tongue position is very helpful in teaching this sound. Give students a physical demonstration of how to make the sound, showing them how the tip of your tongue is placed between your teeth, touching the top teeth. Draw a sketch on the blackboard of the tongue position, or use the symbol for the sound as a visual reminder of the mouth position, with the line across the middle of the symbol θ representing the tongue protruding between the teeth. Unfortunately for the sake of pronunciation, sticking one's tongue out is considered crude, insulting, or embarrassing in many cultures, and students may resist doing this. Although native English speakers do not necessarily pronounce θ with their tongues conspicuously protruding from between their teeth, until they master the sound, students will probably find it easier to produce the correct sound if the tongue position is slightly exaggerated. If possible, have students use small hand mirrors to check their tongue position.

Spend some time practicing the sound θ in isolation before beginning the exercises. Demonstrating how the sound can be sustained, by pronouncing it without stopping for about five seconds, helps students distinguish it from t. Knowing that the sound they are aiming at is a very quiet sound also seems to help students.

Suggested procedures

Practice 1, 2, 3   See Overview, pages 6–7.
Note (Practice 2): Some people pronounce *roof* with the vowel ʊ instead of uw; for these people, *roof* and *Ruth* are not a sound contrast pair.

Contrasts for further practice relevant to student difficulties:

s/θ   sank/thank, sing/thing, sin/thin, saw/thaw, sigh/thigh, seem/theme, sought/thought, mass/math, bass/bath, face/faith, moss/moth, worse/worth

f/θ   fought/thought, frill/thrill, deaf/death, miff/myth

t/θ   taught/thought, team/theme, tin/thin, tick/thick, true/through, mat/math, pat/path, boat/both, boot/booth, debt/death, mitt/myth, fort/fourth, wit/with, brought/broth

Test   See Overview, pages 7–8. *Answers:*
1. thick   2. tanks   3. taught   4. bath   5. sink
6. three.

Practice 4   See Overview, page 8.
Note:

1. Check students' pronunciation of *anything* and *something* (main stress on the first syllable).

2. Pronunciation of *Roths'*: rɔθs.

Dialogue   See Overview, pages 8–9.
Note: was: weak form wəz; strong form wʌz.

Stress   Students practice examples from the dialogue of questions and statements with contrastive stress used to express surprise. In normal English sentence stress, the last important word in the sentence usually has the main stress. If the speaker wants to emphasize something or make a contrast, however, the main stress goes on the information being contrasted or emphasized.

Jumbled sentences   Students practice in pairs. Student A says each sentence, using normal or neutral stress and intonation. Student B gives the appropriate response, putting a strong stress on the part of the sentence that contrasts with what Student A said.

Spelling   See Unit 39.

Further practice

1. Ask students, "What's the opposite of: north [south]; thick [thin]; something [nothing]?"

2. Stress: Students listen to the following sentences read by the teacher and reply to each with this sentence: "Oh, no! The Roths' house is worth thirty thousand dollars." Students should stress the appropriate word as a response to what was said in each case.
a. The Roths' house is worth thirty thousand lire.
b. The Roths' house is worth thirty million dollars.

c. The Roths' house is worth twenty thousand dollars.

d. The Roths' house isn't worth thirty thousand dollars.

e. The Roths' car is worth thirty thousand dollars.

f. The Smiths' house is worth thirty thousand dollars.

Linking pronunciation with other course work

Tie pronunciation in with practice of:

1. Ordinal numbers. Possible contexts for practice include:

a. Birthdays: Students give their birthdays (month and ordinal number); a student at the blackboard writes the dates; after all students have given their birthdays, students try to remember whose birthday was on which date;

b. Using the current page of a calendar to practice dates;

c. Fractions (e.g., in measurements; or students practice reading fractions written in numerals on the blackboard);

d. Results of a race; for example, students use the results of a real race or use a blackboard chart or diagram showing the winners and losers in a race to practice a conversation like the following:

STUDENT A: Who was third?
TEACHER (or STUDENT B): Beth.
STUDENTS: No, she wasn't. She was seventh.

Note: Some ordinal numbers contain very difficult final clusters (e.g., *fifth, sixth*). Even native English speakers often simplify these clusters in some way, such as by pronouncing *fifth* as fɪθ. It is probably best not to insist that students carefully pronounce every sound in these clusters.

2. Directions: Use familiar place names to practice, "Is it north or south of here?" "What direction is it (in)?" (north, south, northeast, etc.);

3. Structures with *anything, something, nothing, everything*;

4. Saying "Thank you";

5. Expressing opinions, beginning with "I think."

Word building

Although *th* is not generally used to form new nouns in modern English, quite a few nouns already exist with this ending. For many of these nouns, there are related words belonging to other parts of speech that do not end in *-th* (often with a change in the vowel as well). Students can practice pairs like the following:

true – truth	long – length
wide – width	strong – strength
deep – depth	warm – warmth
broad – breadth	grow – growth (verb – noun; the others are adjective – noun)

Have students listen to and repeat some or all of these pairs. Then give students sentences in which they choose the correct word in a pair to fill in a blank.

UNIT 39 ð (the feather)

Sound production

See Overview, page 5.

Student difficulties   Nearly all students, except Greek and Spanish speakers, have great difficulty with the sound ð, confusing it with z, d, or sometimes v (pronouncing *then* as *Zen* or *den* or *clothing* as "cloving"). Japanese speakers may also substitute dʒ before the vowel iy or ɪ, saying *this* as "jis." Consonant clusters with ð (as in *bathed* or *bathes*) are particularly troublesome; fortunately, these do not occur very frequently in English. Spanish speakers should not have difficulty producing the sound ð, but since the letter *d* in Spanish is pronounced as d at the beginning of a word and as ð between vowels, they may be confused about the difference between the sounds d and ð in English.

As with the sound θ in Unit 38, showing students the tongue position is very helpful. When practicing the sound in isolation, show how the voice is used to produce ð by moving your hand on your throat. A sustained model of this sound also helps students to distinguish it from d. The sound ð occurs in some very common words like *the, this, that,* and *other.* It is therefore important for students to master it at an early stage.

Suggested procedures

Practice 1, 3   See Overview, pages 6–7.
   Note: Some people pronounce the word *than* with the vowel ɛ. (When unstressed, the vowel is usually ə.)

Practice 2   Students listen and repeat sentences that contrast the sounds ð and z at the beginning of words. (There are very few sound contrast pairs that contrast initial z and ð.)
   Note: Z = ziy in American English, zɛd in British English. Further practice with these and similar questions (e.g., "Whose is this/that?" "Whose are these/those?") can be added, using pictures or objects.
   Contrasts for further practice relevant to student difficulties:
d/ð   Dave/they've, D's/these, den/then, dough/
   though, breeding/breathing, ladder/lather,
   udder/other, wordy/worthy, riding/writhing,
   breed/breathe, load/loathe, sued/soothe
z/ð   Z's/these, Zen/then, rising/writhing, seize/
   seethe, rise/writhe, sues/soothe
   Note: For further practice of initial z/ð, add pairs using nonsense words (e.g., *zoo/thoo*).

Test   See Overview, pages 7–8. *Answers:*
1. day   2. they've   3. teething   4. Z's
5. closing.

Practice 4   See Overview, page 8.
   Other words from the dialogue with the sound ð: than, with (pronounced as either wɪð or wɪθ).

Note: Pronunciation of *clothes:* klowðz or, often, klowz.

Dialogue   See Overview, pages 8–9.

Extension: Students role-play short verbal interchanges used in shopping. For example, bring in or collect from students a number of items (e.g., several pairs of gloves, notebooks, wallets, hats, etc.). Have students practice conversations such as the following:
CUSTOMER: Can I see that scarf?
SALESCLERK: Which one? This one?
CUSTOMER: No. The red one.

CUSTOMER: How much are these gloves?
SALESCLERK: Which ones? These?
CUSTOMER: No. The brown leather ones.
SALESCLERK: $13.95.
CUSTOMER: Can I try them on?

Stress   Students practice stress in sentences. Note that the stress marked in the Student's Book is not the only one possible; for example, *which* in the question might not be stressed, and *I* or *think* in the answer could be stressed. Words like *do, the, is, with,* and *than* would normally not be stressed, however.
   Students listen to and repeat the sentences to the accompaniment of tapping or clapping to demonstrate the stress. Remember that unstressed words generally take less time to say and have vowels that are less clear than stressed words. If students have difficulty with the rhythm or stress, use backward buildup to practice:
others
the others
than the others
better than the others
think
do you think
do you think is better
do you think is better than the others
which jacket
Which jacket do you think is better than the
   others?

Conversation   Students practice in pairs or

groups, as in the model. Check stress. Students should practice the words in the list first. Check the pronunciation of the *-er* (comparative) ending: unstressed ər.

Spelling   The sound ð is written with the letters *th*. Since θ is also spelled with *th*, students may need help predicting when *th* is pronounced θ and when it is pronounced ð. Discuss the following rules, depending on the level of the class:

1. At the beginning of words, *th* is almost always pronounced ð in function ("grammatical") words (e.g., *the, this, these, that, then, there, therefore, they, them, though*). At the beginning of content words (e.g., *think, thing, thirsty, three, thank, thumb, thin*), *th* is pronounced θ.

2. At the end of words, *th* is almost always pronounced θ (exceptions: *with*, which is pronounced wɪθ or wɪð, and *smooth*). If the *th* is followed by *e*, it has the sound ð. The examples in the Student's Book show pairs of related words ending in *th/the* in which the use of a voiceless versus a voiced consonant corresponds with a change in the part of speech. Note that when plural *-s* is added to words ending in *th* (like *path* or *mouth*), the *th* is often pronounced ð.

3. In the middle of a word, *th* can have either the sound ð or θ. It is usually pronounced ð before *er* (e.g., *mother, rather, leather, southern, weather, together, farther*; an exception is *ether*).

Linking pronunciation with other course work

Tie pronunciation in with practice of:

1. *this/that/these/those*; for example, use objects or pictures in the Student's Book and have students ask and answer questions like the following:
A: (pointing to a picture) What are these?
B: They're peas.
A: Are these carrots?
B: No, they aren't.
2. *another/the other*;
3. *I'd rather . . . (than . . .)*;

4. Making comparisons; for example, "This car is bigger than the other one";

5. Talking about family photographs; for example, "This is/that's my mother/father/ brother/grandmother/grandfather";

6. Identifying people in group pictures or photographs; for example, "Which one is your brother?" "The one with the hat/the one on the left/the one with the blond hair," and so on.

Word stress practice

Read the following pairs of words. Have students say whether the stress pattern for each pair was the same or different.
1. together/example [S]   4. dressier/casual [S]
2. attractive/certainly [D] 5. important/another [S]
3. practical/expensive [D] 6. comfortable/ interesting [S]

Either before or after doing this exercise, students should practice the words. Use dots written on the blackboard to illustrate the stress pattern (a large, dark dot for the stressed syllable and smaller, lighter dots for the unstressed syllables) of words that cause difficulty.

UNIT 40 m (mouth)

Sound production

See Overview, page 5.

Student difficulties   Students generally do not have difficulty in pronouncing the sound m, but Spanish, Portuguese, and Japanese speakers may confuse it with n or ŋ at the end of words. Spanish speakers tend to replace m with n or ŋ at the end of words and before consonants not made with the lips – for example, pronouncing *I'm* in *I'm going* as aɪŋ or *some* in *sometimes* with the sound n. Portuguese speakers may strongly nasalize the vowel before m (or other nasal consonants), often making the m itself too weak.

Some students, such as speakers of Lao, may strongly nasalize vowels after m or n. Some students, including speakers of Greek, Italian, and Spanish, may tend to voice s when it is followed by m (as in *smoke*), pronouncing the s more like a z (see Unit 27).

If students have difficulty with final m, emphasize the lip position, and point out that final nasal sounds like m are pronounced clearly in English. In most cases this unit can be taught quickly in preparation for the next unit on n.

Suggested procedures

Practice 1   See Overview, page 8.

Other words from the dialogue with the sound m: me, my, make, some, from, him, um.

Note: Pronunciation of *homemade, Tom Mitchum:* The two m sounds in the middle are pronounced together as one long m.

Dialogue   See Overview, pages 8–9.

If necessary, explain unfamiliar vocabulary. For example:

muffin – a small, often sweet kind of bread
Maine – a state in the northeastern United States (sketch a map)
Mom – informal word for "mother"
homemade – made at home

Intonation   By varying the length and intonation, "mm" (and other nasal sounds, e.g., the sound sometimes written as *unh-unh*, meaning "no") can be used to express various meanings.

Students listen to the conversation on the Cassette, identifying the meaning "mm" has in B's answers. After listening, they should have the chance to practice saying "mm" with the different meanings shown in their books. Write the various "mm"s and their meanings on the blackboard. Ask individual students to choose one of the "mm"s and to say it; other students guess which meaning "mm" had. You may want to add other uses of "mm" or other nasal sounds, such as "Hm!" (I'm surprised); "Mm-hmm" (Yes); "?m?m" [? = a glottal stop] (No); "Um" (hesitation).

Extension   Students look at or listen to the dialogue again and say what meaning each "mm" sound has. (The answers given below are not the only possible interpretations.)

MRS. SMITH: Mm? [= "Yes?" or "What is it?"]
JIM: Mm-hmm. [= "Yes."]
JIM: Oh, um . . . [hesitation]
MRS. SMITH: Mm . . . [= "I'm thinking about that."]

Spelling   The sound m is written with the letter *m*. Note the doubling of *m* to keep the short pronunciation of the vowel in words such as *summer* and *swimming*.

Students often pronounce consonant letters that should be silent. Note the silent *b* in the spelling *mb* in *comb, climb,* and so on, and the silent *n* in the spelling *mn* in *autumn* and *column*. You may also want to add *lm* spellings where the *l* is (for most people) silent, as in *palm* or *calm*. In all these cases, the two consonants together (*mb*, *mn*, and *lm*) have one sound – m. Check to make sure students do not pronounce the silent consonant in these words.

Further practice

Linking sounds between words:
When two m sounds link words, they are pronounced as one long m.
Before f or v (as in *comfortable*), the sound m is often made with the lips and teeth in position for the f or v sound instead of in the usual position for the m sound. Before other sounds, the pronunciation of m does not change; students should pronounce m clearly.
Practice from the blackboard:
Would you like some . . .
    muffins/more/marmalade/milk/mustard/money/
      matches
    fish/veal/food/french fries/vegetables/flowers
    coffee/tea/sugar/cream/cake/toast/cheese/gum/
      grapes/help/water

Note: Pronunciation of *some* here: səm or sm (with syllabic m, where m forms a syllable by itself, with no vowel). If students use a full, stressed vowel, try respelling it on the blackboard as "s'm."

Linking pronunciation with other course work

Tie pronunciation in with practice of:

1. Invitations or commands using the verb *come*: for example, "Come in/Come here/Come with me/Come to my house/Come to the farm/Come home"; or longer forms, such as "Would you like to come swimming/to my house?" (note the rising intonation in the longer form);

2. Questions with *How much/How many*;

3. Object pronouns *him* and *them*;

4. Modal auxiliaries *may*, *might*, *must*; for example, guesses using *must*: "You must be tired/She must be sick/They must have gone," and so on.

Word stress practice

See Overview, pages 11–12.
Recognition Test: A ● • •   B • ● •
1. important [B]   6. comfortable [A]
2. marmalade [A]   7. remember [B]
3. computer [B]   8. tomorrow [B]
4. familiar [B]   9. imagine [B]
5. delicious [B]   10. animal [A]

Some written syllables are not pronounced. Write the list of words below on the blackboard or on a paper handout. Students listen as you say the words and draw a line through the syllable or word part that is not pronounced. *Example:* vegetable.

1. comfortable   5. interesting
2. family   6. different
3. camera   7. natural
4. temperature

Note: The pronunciations of some of these words vary (for example, some people say *family* with three syllables). Include only those words in which *you* drop a syllable.

UNIT 41 n **(nose)**

Sound production

See Overview, page 5.

Student difficulties   Most students do not have trouble with the sound n at the beginnings of words, although some students pronounce it with the tongue touching the top teeth (dental n) rather than with the tongue in back of and not touching the teeth, giving it a slightly foreign sound. Students are more likely to have difficulty with n at the ends of words. Some students, including speakers of Spanish, Portuguese, Japanese, and Turkish, do not pronounce final n clearly enough. They may pronounce the vowel before the n as a nasal vowel, with the n itself disappearing, or they may replace the sound n with m or ŋ, depending on the context. Some Chinese and Thai speakers may replace n with l at the end of words.

Many students have difficulty with syllabic n in words like *garden* or *button*, usually inserting a vowel before the n.

Suggested procedures

Practice 1   See Overview, pages 6–7.
Contrasts for further practice: mice/nice, might/night, meet/neat, moon/noon, mail/nail, met/net, mile/Nile, them/then, some/sun (*or* son), dime/dine, seem/seen, M/N, same/sane, dumb/done, lime/line, mummy/money, dimmer/dinner.

Test   See Overview, pages 7–8. *Answers:*
1. nine   2. cones   3. nice   4. gum   5. name.

Practice 2   See Overview, page 8.
Note: The words *don't* and *can't* are often pronounced with a nasalized vowel instead of a clear n sound.

Most of the words in the bottom part of the list have syllabic n. In such words the n forms a syllable by itself, without any vowel. The tongue goes to the roof of the mouth to make the consonant sound before the n and stays there for n. This happens after a t or d sound: gαrdn, dɪdnt, sɜrtnliy, mαrtn. It may also happen after other sounds: prɪzn, ɪlɛvn, sɛvntiy, lɪsn. It is especially important for students to practice syllabic n after the sounds t and d. The difference between pronunciations with and without syllabic n is more noticeable here than with other sounds; students who are unfamiliar with syllabic n and expect to hear a vowel in words like *garden* or *certainly* may have difficulty understanding these words when said by a native English speaker.

A simplified transcription of some words on the blackboard with stress shown should help students who find syllabic n difficult.

Examples:

● ·   ● ·

gardn   prisn

● ·   ● ·

Martn   sevn

● ·   ● ·

lisn   ofn

Other words from the dialogue with the sound n: no, not, near, morning, in, on, one, than, and, rental, agent, agency, downstairs, want.

Dialogue   See Overview, pages 8–9.

Introduce the situation: Tony Martin is looking for an apartment. Check students' understanding of "rental agency" and "rental agent."

Extension   Additional practice, especially of syllabic n: Ask yes/no questions about the dialogue. Students respond, using short answers: "No, he didn't/No, he isn't," and so on. (Include some questions for which the answer is "yes.") For example:

Is Tony Martin looking for a house in the country?
Does he want an apartment with two bedrooms?
Is the apartment in the dialogue furnished?
Does the apartment have a kitchen?
Does the kitchen have an oven?
Can tenants use the garden?
Could Tony watch TV after midnight?
Did Tony rent the apartment?

Game   Students should first practice saying some or all of the numbers. Check that they say the final n clearly in numbers like *nine* and *eleven*. If necessary, review the difference in stress between numbers like *seventeen* and *seventy* (see Unit 2). Note that stress affects the pronunciation of t in many of these numbers:

In stressed *-teen* (17, 19, etc.), t is voiceless and aspirated.

In unstressed *-ty* (30, 90, etc.), t has the sound of voiced flap t (see Unit 23).

In *twenty*, the t is often not pronounced: twɛniy.

Students play in groups of about five people. The person who calls out the numbers should check them off as they are called, without letting the other students see them.

For further practice at another time, mini bingo could be played using higher numbers (e.g., 979, 720, 107).

Spelling

1. Note the doubling of *n* after short vowels in words like *penny*, *dinner*, and *running*. Compare the pronunciation of words like *diner/dinner*.

2. Silent letters: Make sure students do not pronounce the letter *k* or *g* in the combinations *kn* and *gn*; draw a line or an X through the silent letter if necessary. (Less commonly, the combination *pn* may also have the sound n: *pneumonia, pneumatic*.)

3. Introduce the idea of *homophones* – words that sound alike but are spelled differently. Demonstrate with pairs like *know/no, see/sea, meet/meat,* or *mail/male*. On the blackboard, write the first word in pairs like those below; students, working alone or in pairs, try to find a homophone for each one. (You may want to allow students to use their dictionaries.)

Example: know
          Homophone: no

knows – nose	sun – son
knot – not	won – one
knew – new	none – nun
knight – night	scene – seen

4. Spelling patterns for syllabic n:

n didn't, hadn't, couldn't, hasn't, isn't

en garden, frighten, listen, student, often, sudden, written

on button, person, lesson, cotton

in Latin

ain certainly, mountain, curtain

an important

ion station, television

Linking pronunciation with other course work

Tie pronunciation in with practice of:

1. Negative short answers using "No . . . isn't/ doesn't/haven't/hasn't/didn't/shouldn't/ couldn't," etc. (Note the practice of syllabic n.) For example, students give short answers to questions about a picture, such as the one in Unit 34.)

2. Asking and talking about abilities, using *can* and *can't*: "Can you swim/speak German?" etc.

3. Negative questions and tag questions (see, for example, Units 12 and 20).

4. Present perfect with past participles ending in *-en* (*taken, been*, etc.); for example, students practice, substituting phrases like the following, from the blackboard or a paper handout:

Have you ever ridden a horse/eaten snails/ written a song/driven a truck/gotten a prize/ given a speech in English/spoken to a famous person/fallen asleep in class?

Students ask and answer questions (A: "Have you ever ridden a horse?" B: "Yes, I have./No, I haven't."), circulating around the room until they have found other students who have done each of the things listed. Students should practice the past participles first (note that syllabic n occurs in all these past participles except *spoken* and *fallen*).

Word stress practice

See Overview, pages 11–12.

● ● ● avenue, agency, certainly, seventy, sentences

● ● ● apartment, forbidden, eleven, beginning, good morning

● ● ● seventeen, twenty-one, ninety-nine, understand, introduce

UNIT 42 ŋ (ring)

Sound production

See Overview, page 5.

Note: The sound ŋ does not occur at the beginning of words in English.

Variation In informal speech, people often pronounce the *-ing* verb ending, as in *sleeping, laughing*, or *doing*, as ɪn rather than ɪŋ.

Student difficulties The sound ŋ occurs frequently, especially in the present continuous tense. Although mistakes rarely cause confusion in meaning, they are quite noticeable. Arabic, French, some German, Farsi, Greek, Hebrew, Italian, Turkish, West African, and Slavic speakers may have difficulty with this sound, usually pronouncing it ŋg, ŋk, or n. Some students may pronounce it as n + g because of the spelling.

For students who add g or k to ŋ, it sometimes helps to get them to sing the sound (in, say, the word *sing*) and end it by gradually getting softer. It may also help them to practice words such as *longer* and *thinker*, gradually slowing down the pronunciation and increasing the gap between the first and second syllables.

Whereas some students tend to add a g after every ŋ sound, speakers of Dutch and German tend to omit g after ŋ where it should be pronounced, as in *hunger, finger*, or *longer*. Portuguese speakers may strongly nasalize the vowel before a nasal consonant (m, n or ŋ), leaving the final consonant itself very indistinct. Spanish speakers may replace other nasal sounds with ŋ, or vice versa, depending on what sounds surround it (also see Units 40 and 41). They may also tend to drop the k after ŋ in words like *think*, creating confusion between words like *thing* and *think*.

Suggested procedure

Practice 1 and 2   See Overview, pages 6–7.

Contrasts for further practice relevant to student difficulties:

n/ŋ sun/sung, ton/tongue, sin/sing, lawn/long, fan/fang, hand/hanged, banning/banging, sinning/singing, sinner/singer

ŋk/ŋ sank/sang, stink/sting, rank/rang, tank/tang, sinking/singing

Test   See Overview, pages 7–8. *Answers:*
1. rink   2. banged   3. sinks   4. ban   5. singers.

Practice 3   See Overview, page 8.

Note: In the words *finger* and *angrily*, the *ng* is pronounced ŋg. In words like *singing, bringing, hanging,* or *singer,* however, where the *-ing* or *-er* ending is added to a verb that ends in the sound ŋ (e.g., *sing* sɪŋ), the *ng* spelling in the middle of the word is pronounced ŋ by most speakers: sɪŋər, sɪŋɪŋ. Make sure students do not add a g sound in these words.

Other words from the dialogue with the sound ŋ: doing, looking, putting, falling, holding, shouting, helping, sleeping, going (though note that *going to,* with reference to the future, is often pronounced gənə).

Dialogue   See Overview, pages 8–9. See below, under Conversation.

Conversation   Students practice wh-questions and the sound ŋ in the present continuous tense. Check that they use falling intonation in the wh-questions. Also check stress in the verbs ending in *-ing.* Since students are concentrating on the ŋ sound in this unit, they may tend to overstress the last syllable of these words. The *-ing* syllable should not be stressed. Tap with a ruler to show the stress, or write words on the blackboard, putting the stressed syllables in large capitals and the unstressed syllables in very small letters.

Students ask and answer questions about the pictures, as in the example, either in pairs or as a whole class. Encourage them to do this without referring back to the dialogue.

Note that the dialogue and the questions provide practice with the nasal sounds m and n as well as ŋ. If students tend to confuse these sounds, ask additional questions about the dialogue that elicit answers with these sounds (e.g., "What time is it?"). Or, have students practice the dialogue, working in small groups. They can then act it out, providing appropriate sound effects.

Spelling   The sound ŋ is usually written with the letters *ng* or, before a k or g sound, with the letter *n.*

The letters *ng* can represent either the single sound ŋ (as in *ring*) or the sounds ŋ + g (as in *anger* or *English*). Note that when the comparative and superlative endings *-er* and *-est* are added to adjectives or adverbs (*younger, longest*), a g sound is added in the pronunciation: *Young* is pronounced as yʌŋ, *younger* as yʌŋgər. This does not happen when endings are added to verbs: *ringing* rɪŋɪŋ, *singer* sɪŋər.

Linking pronunciation with other course work

Tie pronunciation in with practice of:

1. Continuous tenses with *-ing* verb endings; for example:

a. asking and answering questions about a picture showing several people doing different activities ("What's X doing?" "What are X and Y doing?" "Who's [watching television]?");

b. asking and answering questions about the future: "What will you be doing at 9 o'clock tonight/this time tomorrow, etc.?" "I'll (probably) be . . .";

c. asking and answering questions about people students know: "What is your husband/wife/daughter/son/sister doing now?" Or, use a hypothetical time: "It's 8 o'clock. What is your wife/husband/mother . . . probably doing now?"

2. Asking and talking about preferences in sports and other leisure activities: "Do you like swimming/playing tennis/watching football/dancing/playing ping pong?" etc.

3. Complaining about problems in an apartment or in a house; for example, "There's something wrong with my kitchen sink/my refrigerator/the intercom," or "The kitchen sink is dripping/The ceiling is falling down/The paint is peeling/My refrigerator isn't working."

4. Greetings ("Good morning/Good afternoon/Good evening/Good night") or times of day, such as in:

A: Come (downtown, to the movies, etc.) with me tomorrow.

B: What time?

A: Nine/one/eleven/seven o'clock.

B: In the morning?

A: No. In the evening/afternoon.

(Greetings and times of day practice all the nasal consonants.)

5. Structures with *anything, something, nothing, everything*.

Word stress practice

Review the usual stress pattern of:

1. Words ending in *-ing*:

● • morning, singing, banging, holding, doing, standing, shouting, running, sleeping

2. Words ending in *-er/-or*:

● • singer, neighbor, finger, Mr., hammer, ladder, answer, longer

UNIT 43 | Part 1 (letter)

Sound production

See Overview, page 5.

Note: The instructions in the Student's Book describe the production of "clear l" as it is usually pronounced at the beginning of a word.

Variation There are two kinds of l sound in English. At the beginning of a word or between vowels, especially before vowels made in the front of the mouth (as in *leave, live, late, left, lamb*), l usually has a clear, light sound. At the end of a word or before a consonant (as in *pull* or *old*), l has a darker, heavier sound. This sound is made with the front of the tongue in the same position as for clear l, but with the back of the tongue raised. Many people also use a darker l before vowels made in the back of the mouth (as in *look* or *low*). (British speakers make a sharper distinction between clear l and dark l than American speakers, using clear l at the beginning of all words and dark l at the end of words or before consonants.)

Student difficulties Speakers of Vietnamese, Thai, and Lao have difficulty distinguishing n and l at the end of words. They usually substitute n for l, for example, pronouncing *tell* as *ten*. Some Chinese speakers also confuse n and l. Speakers of Chinese, Japanese, Thai, and other Asian languages, as well as speakers of some African languages, tend to confuse r and l (see Unit 45). Students who have trouble with l tend to have particular difficulty with it in consonant clusters (as in *glass, slow,* or *cold*) or in final position (as in *feel* or *pull*). Even students who do not otherwise have problems with l may have difficulty with it in these positions. Many students, such as those who speak Arabic, Turkish, Farsi, Indian languages, African languages, Japanese, Chinese, and Thai, tend to insert a vowel between consonants in a cluster. (Dutch speakers may insert a vowel in some final clusters, such as in *milk* or *film*.) Some students may drop one of the consonants in clusters, especially in final clusters (e.g., dropping the l in *cold*). Sometimes students (e.g., speakers of Portuguese) replace l in final position or before a consonant with a sound resembling ʊ. Some students (e.g., speakers of Chinese) may drop a final l or add a vowel after it. Syllabic l (l pronounced as a syllable by itself, without any vowel, as in *bottle*) often causes particular difficulty. Students (e.g., speakers of French) often add a vowel – sometimes a full, stressed vowel – before the l.

Many languages have only one l sound, either clear l or dark l; speakers of these languages will tend to use the sound found in their language in all positions in English. Speakers of French, German, Farsi, and Scandinavian and Indian languages, for example, tend to use clear l only.

Other languages, such as Russian, Turkish, and Dutch, have both sounds, but not in the same places as in English. Students who speak those languages may substitute dark l for clear l or vice versa. Many students pronounce l with the tongue in a slightly different position than for English l (e.g., further forward or back in the mouth), giving it a foreign sound. (For English l the front of the tongue is just behind the top teeth.) The use of only clear l or dark l, the substitution of one l sound in place of the other, or the use of a non-English l will not cause misunderstandings, but will contribute to an accent different from that of a native English speaker.

Suggested procedures

Practice 1   See Overview, pages 6–7.
   Contrasts for further practice: not/lot, knee/Lee, nap/lap, nice/lice, knit/lit, knock/lock, niece/lease, snacks/slacks, snob/slob, Jenny/jelly, tenor/teller, winning/willing.

Test   See Overview, pages 7–8. *Answers:*
1. line   2. no   3. collect   4. snowball   5. night.

Practice 2, 3, and 4   See Overview, page 8.
   In each section, students listen to and repeat the captions for the illustrations as recorded on the Cassette or read by the teacher. Then they answer the questions next to the picture (the teacher or a student should read the questions aloud).
   Each section practices the sound l in a different position: at the beginning of words (Practice 2), in the middle of words (Practice 3), and in consonant clusters (Practice 4). Students may have particular difficulty with l following an r sound, as in *early*, or in consonant clusters. If necessary, practice from the blackboard. For example:
llllack   bllllack   black
llllass   gllllass   glass

   Other words from the dialogue with the sound l: later, like, love, I'll.

Dialogue   See Overview, pages 8–9.
   Note: Some students find the pronunciation of *would you like* difficult, often dropping the d or pronouncing the silent l in *would*. If they pronounce the l, show them that *would* is pronounced like *wood*. Native English speakers often blend the first two words: wʊdʒə.

Extension   Students role-play ordering in a restaurant. Other foods with the sound l that could be added include liver, lasagna, leeks, lemon, lobster, clams, plums, blueberries, chocolate, vanilla, chili, broccoli, cauliflower, and celery.

Spelling   See Unit 44.

Further practice

1. If students have difficulty with l in consonant clusters, provide extra practice using a drill like the following.
Example:
TEACHER: That plate is black, isn't it?
STUDENT: Yes, it's a black plate.
Words for substitution (in place of *plate/black*):
flower/blue	plan/clever
glass/clean	flower/plastic
plane/slow	class/clever
clock/plastic	class/sleepy

2. Students talk about likes and dislikes, making sentences (from blackboard cues) beginning, "I like/love/don't like:"
lamb/lettuce/lemonade/liver/salad/melon/olives/garlic/chocolate
flying/sleeping late/complaining/telling lies/traveling/cleaning/playing tennis/climbing cliffs

Linking pronunciation with other course work

Tie pronunciation in with practice of:
1. The greeting "Hello";
2. Requests with *please*;
3. Telling the time using *o'clock*;
4. Questions with *long*; for example, "How long have you lived here?" "Have you lived here for a long time?"

Word stress practice

See Overview, pages 11–12.
Recognition Test: A • •   B • •

1. lettuce [A]
2. olives [A]
3. salad [A]
4. collect [B]
5. melon [A]

6. color [A]
7. o'clock [B]
8. complain [B]
9. hello [B]
10. waitress [A]

UNIT 44 | Part 2 (ball)

Sound production

See Overview, page 5.

The sound l in the words practiced in this unit often has a slightly different sound than in the words practiced in Unit 43. Tell students to say l. Explain that as they say l, they should raise the back of the tongue closer to the roof of the mouth, keeping the front of the tongue in the same place. This describes the production of "dark l," as it is usually pronounced at the end of a word or before a consonant.

Note: Some speakers produce this sound with the whole tongue a little further back in the mouth than for clear l.

Student difficulties   See Unit 43.

Many students have particular difficulty with l in final position or before another consonant, as in *fall* or *hold*. If students tend to drop final l or replace it with a vowel, have them check the position of their tongues as they finish saying words like *I'll* or *pull*. The front of the tongue should be touching the roof of the mouth just behind the front teeth.

If students have difficulty producing dark l, tell them to say the sound l and, as they say l, to try to say the sound uw. Some native English speakers add a slight ə sound when l comes after a front vowel like iy or ey (as in *feel* or *tail*), as the tongue moves from the front of the mouth to dark l. It may be easier for students to achieve the correct l sound if they add this ə.

Many students have difficulty with syllabic l, as in *bottle*, where l forms a syllable by itself, without any vowel. As with syllabic n, practice of syllabic l is most important after the sounds t and d, as in *little* or *candle*. To make syllabic l after these sounds, the tongue goes to the roof of the mouth for t or d and then stays there for l, with the air for t or d escaping over the sides of the tongue as l is pronounced. Note that t is usually a voiced sound before syllabic l. Writing words in a modified phonetic script on the blackboard may be helpful in practicing syllabic l: **littl**, **bicycl**, **uncl**, and so on. If the syllabic l is after a t or d, tell students not to move their tongues away from the roof of the mouth between t/d and l. Some students may replace syllabic l with a clear l without making a separate syllable; for these students, write "**littəl**," "**bicycəl**," "**uncəl**," and so on. Indicate the stressed syllable on the blackboard; check that students do not stress the final syllable in these words.

Suggested procedures

Practice 1   See Overview, pages 6–7.
Contrasts for further practice: in/ill, win/will, mine/mile, rain/rail, Ben/bell, mean/meal, been/bill, fine/file, fin/fill, main/mail, phone/foal, even/evil, earn/earl.

Test   See Overview, pages 7–8. *Answers:*
1. pin   2. bowl   3. in.

Practice 2   See Overview, page 8. The words in the list usually have the sound dark l.
Other words from the dialogue with the sound l: please, telling. (These have the sound l practiced in Unit 43.)

Dialogue   See Overview, pages 8–9.

Intonation   Here students practice intonation in exclamations and echo questions. Exclamations generally use a wider range of pitch than ordinary statements, with the voice often rising to a high tone on the last stress and then falling. In echo questions, the voice starts at a fairly high pitch and then rises even higher. Sometimes the voice falls before it rises at the end. Intonation may vary, depending on the purpose of the echo question: for example, to express amazement or surprised disagreement, to request repetition or confirmation, etc.

Conversation   Students practice exclamations and echo questions, as in the example, choosing adjectives from the list to describe the pictures below. Students should practice the adjectives and the words under the pictures first. If necessary, check that students understand the meanings of the adjectives. For example, ask them to find a word in the list that has the same meaning as *small*; words in the list whose meanings are the opposite of those of *horrible* and *difficult*. Or, ask students to find two words in the list that have the same meaning (*small/little*) and pairs of words that have opposite meanings (*simple/difficult*; *wonderful/horrible*). Answers here might vary; *horrible* and *miserable*, for example, may be considered to have similar meanings.

Spelling

1. Doubling of *l*: Note that *l* is often doubled at the end of a word after a short vowel, as in *bell* (compare *bed*) or the vowels ɔ and ʊ (as in *fall* and *pull*).

   In American English, when *-ed* or *-ing* is added to a verb ending in *l*, the *l* is doubled only if the vowel before it is stressed (i.e., the spelling rules are the same as for other letters). In British English, the *l* is doubled even if the vowel is not stressed (American: *traveled, traveling*; British: *travelled, travelling*).

2. Spelling of syllabic l:
le   little, candle, apple, table, uncle, bicycle, example, puzzle
al, el, il, ol   final, travel, pencil, symbol

3. Silent *l*: Many students pronounce *l* where it should be silent; others may drop *l* in consonant clusters where it should be pronounced. For later review, give students a list of words such as the following. Have them either listen as you read the words aloud or just look at the words in written form. They should indicate which words are pronounced with the sound l.

1. could	6. cold
2. talk	7. half
3. milk	8. chalk
4. calm*	9. help
5. felt	10. yolk

*Note: Some people pronounce the *l* here.

Further practice

1. Use the words and pictures from the conversation to practice the final consonant cluster lz in words with syllabic l + plural ending z, following a model such as the following:

Examples:
A: That bottle is small.
B: Those bottles are all small.
A: This table is beautiful.
B: These tables are all beautiful.

If necessary, practice from the blackboard first, using modified phonetic script: write, for example, ''bottlz,'' ''tablz,'' and so on. Pronunciation of *are all*: ər ɔl.

2. Practice talking about likes and dislikes, with students making sentences (using blackboard cues) beginning: ''I don't like/like/love...''

large	planes/televisions/pencils/pills/hotels/flowers
black	walls/telephones/glasses/plates/tables/olives/bicycles
cold	meals/pools/apples/milk/hotels/people
old	bottles/films/tables/plates/buildings/hotels/people

Example:
[Blackboard cue: *large*]
TEACHER: hotels
STUDENT: I don't like large hotels.

Linking pronunciation with other course work

Tie pronunciation in with practice of:

1. The use of adjectives in descriptions: *small, old, clean, yellow, black, blue, clever, slow, full, cold, little, difficult, simple, careful, sensible, wonderful,* etc.;

2. Asking and talking about the future, using *will*;

3. *myself/yourself/herself/himself,* etc.

Word stress practice

See Overview, pages 11–12.

● •   uncle, careful, special, simple, candle, puzzle, circle, table, bottle, people

● • •   beautiful, difficult, bicycle, gentleman, wonderful, sensible, horrible, miserable, comfortable, hospital

UNIT 45   r Part 1 (rain)

Note: This unit practices r before vowels.

Sound production

See Overview, page 5.

Student difficulties   Almost all students have difficulty with the English sound r. Speakers of many Asian languages confuse l and r, particularly Chinese, Japanese, Thai, and Lao speakers. Speakers of Japanese, for example, usually substitute the Japanese r, a "flap" sound, for both; Thai speakers tend to substitute l for r. Speakers of some African (especially West African) languages may also confuse l and r.

French, German, Danish, Hebrew, Portuguese, and many Dutch speakers often make a sound produced too far back in the mouth (uvular r). At the beginning of words, Portuguese speakers may use a voiceless sound that sounds like a strong h.

Many students (such as speakers of Arabic, Farsi, Greek, Italian, Portuguese, Spanish, Turkish, Norwegian, and Swedish, as well as speakers of African, Indian, and Slavic languages) trill r or pronounce it as a short flap sound resembling the d in *ladder*.

A trilled or flapped r does not prevent students from being understood. The sound does, in fact, occur in some varieties of English (such as in Scottish English). It is, however, a noticeable part of a foreign accent, and if students want to sound "native," the English r sound must be mastered. Students' use of a trilled or flapped r is also likely to interfere with their ability to pronounce vowels before r correctly (see Unit 46).

Uvular r also does not cause misunderstandings in meaning. But the sound r occurs so frequently that it can be distracting to listen to English pronounced in this way. Demonstration of the correct tongue position and practice of the l/r sound contrast pairs should help students to use the front of the tongue rather than the back.

Confusing l and r causes many misunderstandings in meaning and is an aspect of a foreign accent that is often subject to ridicule. Students tend to have particular difficulty when r is in a consonant cluster or in a word that also has an l sound. Note that with l the air passes over the sides of the tongue; with r the air moves over the center of the tongue. This can be felt if the tongue is held in position for the sound and the breath is sharply inhaled.

A less common problem among nonnative speakers is confusion of r with w. Tell students who substitute w for r to make the sound with their tongues, not just their lips; the lips also should not form so tight a circle.

In correcting all problems with r, it is important to spend time practicing the correct mouth position. Demonstrate the tongue position, emphasizing that the front of the tongue must not touch the roof of the mouth for r (this is especially useful for students who use a trilled or flapped r or who confuse l and r). The tongue is curled slightly back, and the sides of the tongue touch the upper back teeth, forming a hollow space in the middle of the tongue. The lips are pushed forward a little into a circle. (*Note:* This describes the mouth position most speakers use for initial r. In the middle of a word, as in *parent*, the tongue may point up without being curled back and the lips may not be rounded.)

Begin practice of r in contexts where it is easiest for students to make the correct mouth position. The tongue position is easier after a vowel like ɑ, which is made with the tongue in a similar position, than after a vowel like ɛ. Lip rounding is most likely to occur automatically before a vowel like ow or uw. Have students start by saying the sound ɑ. Tell them to move their tongues up slowly as they say ɑ and curl the tip of the tongue back – but without touching the roof of the mouth. Now tell them to make this r sound longer and then say uw: ɑrrrrruw. After they have practiced doing this, they should try dropping the ɑ part.

Clusters with r often cause students particular difficulty. The combination gr may be the easiest to start with, because the tongue position for g is closest to the position for r. Have students say the sound g. Then, with the tongue almost in the same position, they should stop touching the back of the mouth with the tongue and point the front of the tongue toward the roof of the mouth (or curl the front of the tongue slightly back) and make their lips round: grrrr. When forming consonant clusters with r, the mouth often starts to form an r while making the first sound. Tell students to try saying both sounds at the same time.

Suggested procedures

Practice 1   See Overview, pages 6–7.
Contrasts for further practice relevant to student difficulties:
l/r lock/rock, low/row, load/road, led/red, lied/ride, law/raw, lice/rice, lime/rhyme, lane/rain, loyal/royal, lip/rip, lace/race, late/rate, liver/river, lead/read, list/wrist, collect/correct, jelly/Jerry, belly/berry, elect/erect, alive/arrive,

palace/Paris, flute/fruit, flame/frame, flight/fright, flea/free, play/pray, bleed/breed, bland/brand, cloud/crowd, clown/crown, climb/crime, glow/grow, glue/grew, glamour/grammar
w/r wing/ring, wide/ride, which/rich, waist/raced, wink/rink, ways/raise, way/ray, wait/rate, won/run, west/rest, went/rent, wise/rise

Test   See Overview, pages 7–8. *Answers:*
1. long   2. collect   3. grass   4. pilot   5. right.

Practice 2 and 3   See Overview, page 8.
Other words from the dialogue with the sound r: French, Paris.
Note:
1. The words in Practice 3 contain both l and r sounds.
2. Words in which r is not followed by a vowel (*are, where, girl, over, ever, other, computer, working, hardly*) have not been included for practice in this unit.

Dialogue   See Overview, pages 8–9.
Point out the use of "Really?" in the dialogue to show polite interest. English speakers tend to use conversational fillers like this quite often to show that they are listening and interested. Have students briefly practice. Tell them things, either true or imaginary (especially surprising things), about yourself or students in the class; students respond with "Really?"

Conversation   Working in pairs, students ask and answer questions, as in the examples, substituting names and occupations in any order from the list. Student B should answer using the information given in the dialogue.
Pronunciation: Rose's rowzɪz, Chris's krɪsɪz.
Note that the pronunciation of the possessive 's ending follows the same rules as the pronunciation of -s/-es plural and third-person singular present tense verb endings (see Unit 28).

Spelling   The sound r is usually written with the letter *r*, or, in the middle of words, with *rr* (*rr* also occurs at the end of a few uncommon words). At the beginning of a word it is sometimes spelled *wr* or *rh*, with the *w* or *h* silent.

Further practice

Practice with antonyms that have the sounds r and l. Give students one of the words in pairs such as the following. Students think of a word that has the opposite meaning.

right/wrong   late/early
short/long (*or* tall)   large/small
light/dark   simple/difficult
interesting/dull (*or* boring) married/single
ugly/pretty (*or* beautiful)

Linking pronunciation with other course work

Tie pronunciation in with practice in:

1. Talking about colors. The following give practice in the sounds l and r: red, green, gray, brown, orange, cream, purple, yellow, blue, black, lilac, lavender, light blue, pale yellow, etc. For example, students say what their favorite color is or find objects in the room that are the colors listed above.

2. Talking about occupations.

3. Replies to "How are you?": *"All right."/"Pretty good."*

Word stress practice

See Overview, pages 11–12.
Recognition test:
A ● • •   B • ● •   C • ● • •   D • • ● •
1. computer [B]   6. interesting [A]
2. librarian [C]   7. receptionist [C]
3. somebody [A]   8. electrician [D]
4. reporter [B]   9. photographer [C]
5. occupation [D]   10. America [C]

Practice stress patterns in words when suffixes are added to them. (Adapt the selection of words to suit the level of the class.) Often when we add a suffix (like *-ist*), the stress in the word stays on the same syllable.

Students listen and repeat:
bi**o**logy   bi**o**logist
psy**cho**logy   psy**cho**logist
op**tom**etry   op**tom**etrist
e**con**omy   e**con**omist
science   **sci**entist
re**ceive**   re**cep**tionist

(Note the change in sounds in *receive – receptionist*. The placement of the stress remains the same, however.)

Suffixes that do not cause a shift in stress include *-er* (drive/driver, report/reporter) and *-ess* (wait/waitress, act/actress). But other times when we add a suffix, like *-ian*, the stress moves to a different syllable. Students listen and repeat:
music   mu**si**cian
e**lec**tric   elec**tri**cian
politics   poli**ti**cian
mathe**mat**ics   mathema**ti**cian
library   li**brar**ian

Point out that the stress moves to the syllable before the *-ian* suffix (and note the pronunciation of *-cian*: ʃən).

UNIT 46 r Part 2 (here)

Note: This unit practices r after vowels.

Sound production

See Overview, page 5.

When the sound r follows a vowel in the same syllable in a word, it often affects the way the vowel is pronounced.

Note: Many people make the sound r a little differently after a vowel. Some do not curl the tongue back. Instead, they bunch up the tongue in the middle toward the roof of the mouth or pull it back a little.

Variation   There is a great deal of dialect variation in the pronunciation of vowels before r. Different speakers may use different sets of vowels before r or pronounce the vowels differently. Some speakers, for example, pronounce the word *hear* with a vowel more like ɪ; others use a vowel closer to iy; still others may use a sound somewhere between iy and ɪ. Similar variation occurs between ɛ and ey in the word *there* and ʊ and uw in *poor*. Some people use three different vowels in the words *Mary, merry,* and *marry*; many people pronounce all three words with the same vowel (ɛ, or a vowel close to this). Some people pronounce *for* and *four* with different vowels, but many use the same vowel (ɔ). Note, too, that many people add a slight ə sound between a vowel and a following r, such as in *here, poor, there,* and especially in words with diphthongs, such as *fire* or *hour*. As with other sounds, it is probably best for students to follow the pronunciation model of their teacher.

Note: British speakers (and some American speakers) pronounce r only when it comes before a vowel. They do not pronounce r before a consonant or a pause (as in *airport* or *here*). For these speakers, r would be silent in most of the words in this unit.

Student difficulties
Almost all students have difficulty with r and the way it affects the pronunciation of a preceding vowel. They commonly substitute an r sound from their own language, replace r with l, or drop r after a vowel.

Have students practice r after a vowel, starting with ɑ (as described in Unit 45). They should then practice this using different vowels. In each case, students should make sure that they do not touch the roof of their mouths with their tongues. See Unit 45 for further discussion of student difficulties and suggestions for teaching r.

If students have previously practiced the sounds ər or ɜr, it should be easier for them to pronounce the vowels here correctly. Tell them to say the sound ər or ɜr (see Units 8 and 20) after each of the vowels practiced in this unit; this should help them to make the correct sound.

Students may need practice in:
1. distinguishing final l and final r;
2. distinguishing words with a vowel + r in the

same syllable from words with no r after the vowel;
3. distinguishing various vowels before r from others (e.g., the vowels in *here* and *there*); spelling difficulties often add to students' confusion in such cases.

Suggested procedures

Practice 1 and 2   See Overview, pages 6–7.
Note: The exact words that form sound contrast pairs here will be different for different speakers, depending on what vowel sounds they use before r. For many speakers, for example, the words *hill/here* and *tell/tear* (verb) would more likely be sound contrast pairs than the pairs given in the Student's Book.

Contrasts for further practice relevant to student difficulties:
l/r feel/fear, real/rear, we'll/we're; fill/fear, hill/here, will/we're; pail/pair, fail/fair; tell/tear (verb), bell/bear, well/wear, fell/fair; wall/war, Paul/pour, tall/tore; pole/pour, stole/store; pool/poor, tool/tour; pull/poor; tile/tire, while/wire; owl/hour

vowel/vowel + r E/ear, bead/beard, tea/tear (noun), bee/beer; bid/beard; day/dare, pays/pears, stayed/stared; shed/shared; cot/cart, hot/heart, dock/dark; caught/court, sauce/source, saw/sore; coat/court, sew/sore; shut/shirt (and see Unit 20); lose/lures

Some contrasting vowels before r:
ear/air, hear/hair, tear (noun)/tear (verb), cheers/chairs, dear/dare, beer/bear, fear/fair
hair/her, fair/fur, stair/stir, pair/purr
care/car, fair/far, stair/star, scare/scar, bear/bar
(For contrasts of other vowels, see Units 10 and 20.)

Test   See Overview, pages 7–8. *Answers:*
1. fire   2. Fall   3. towers   4. cot   5. cheers
6. tours.

Practice 3   See Overview, page 8. *Note:* The words in the Student's Book are arranged in columns by vowel sound.

Other words from the dialogue with r following a vowel: hear, dear, we're, downstairs, airline, very, marvelous, sir, were, short, store, morning, New York, tomorrow, sorry, toward, our, are, never, over, passengers.

Dialogue See Overview, pages 8–9.

Before students listen to the dialogue, call attention to the illustration. Ask questions about the information shown ("What is the number of the flight?" "What time will it leave?" etc.). Tell students that the people in the dialogue are passengers on this flight. Have students then listen to the dialogue with their books closed. You may want to play the Cassette more than once.

Practice 4 Students practice requests for directions and answers: rising intonation for the question, falling intonation for the answer. The person asking for information starts by saying "Excuse me"; this is sometimes said at a fairly high pitch or with a slight rising tone at the end, to show politeness or friendliness. Polite requests for information may also start at a fairly high pitch.

Note that in the answer to the first question, the word *there* occurs twice. The first *there*, used to introduce a sentence where the real subject follows ("There's a cafeteria downstairs"), is unstressed and in rapid speech might be said with the vowel ə. The second *there* is an adverb of place ("over there") that contrasts with *here* and is stressed.

Conversation Students practice asking for and giving directions, either in pairs or larger groups, first practicing the words for substitution. (Check students' understanding of the words.) Review the stress pattern for noun compounds (strong stress on the first element, lighter stress on the second) in words used here and elsewhere in the unit; for example: **air**port, **air**line, **book**store, de**part**ment store, **hard**ware store, **tour**ist office, **hair**dresser, **su**permarket, **fire** alarm.

Contrast this with the stress pattern for *downstairs* and *upstairs*, which are used in B's replies (strong stress on the second element, lighter stress on the first).

Spelling *Note:* See also Unit 9 (ɑr), Unit 10 (ɔr), and Unit 20 (ɜr). The variety and overlapping of spellings for vowels before r is very confusing for students, especially since some spellings represent sounds before r that they do not represent in other places. Some of the spellings shown in the Student's Book for each sound are, of course, more common than others. The spellings *ear, eer, ere,* and *ier,* for example, regularly spell the sound ɪ/iy + r, while the spelling *er* (which can spell the sound ɛ/ey before r as well as ɪ/iy) is probably more common as a spelling for ɜr. In the spellings listed under ɛ/ey + r, note that some people say some of the words spelled with *ar(r)* with the vowel æ. The spellings *ere, ear, er,* and *ar* are irregular spellings for the sound ɛ/ey; the first two more commonly spell ɪ/iy + r, and the last more commonly spells ɑr (as in *far*).

To review the spellings of vowels before r, give students a list of words to sort by sound. Give them a list written on paper or on the blackboard or prepare a group activity using cards. (See instructions in Unit 6, under Spelling Review.) Sample words, to be given in scrambled order:
hear, here, near, clearly, year
wear, there, stairs, care, their
were, early, word, bird, heard, learn
heart, hard, start, large
warm, four, more, short, store

Linking pronunciation with other course work

Tie pronunciation in with practice of:

1. Asking for and giving directions: "Where?" "Over there/right here/near . . ./around the corner," etc. Practice the contrast of l and r in *left/ right/straight ahead;*

2. Possessive pronouns: *her, your, our, their;*

3. "Would you like some more . . . ?" in offering things; "Here you are" when giving something to someone;

4. Vocabulary used in looking for an apartment; for example:

a. Students look at classified ads and match abbreviations with full forms: BR (bedroom), LR (living room), A/C (air-conditioning), lge (large), nr (near), elev (elevator), etc.

b. Students role-play calling about an apartment advertised for rent. (Note instances of l/r: living room/bedroom/etc., large/small/rent/utilities/security deposit.) For example:
I'm calling about the apartment for rent./ Is it still available?/ How much is the rent?/ How many rooms are there?/ Is there a separate kitchen?/ Is the apartment near . . . ?/ Does the rent include utilities?

5. Describing people and what they are wearing:
   dress/shirt/skirt (pleated/straight/full)/scarf/
      sweater/blouse/sleeves/belt/glasses
   striped/plaid/print/solid/flowered/wool/short/
      long
   colors (see Unit 45, under Linking Pronunciation . . .): add "dark" (blue, green, etc.)

For example: Tell students to look around the room at their classmates and remember as much about them as possible. After a minute or two, ask one student to come to the front of the room and face away from the class. Choose another student; ask the student at the front to describe what that student is wearing. Repeat this, with other students coming to the front of the room.

Word stress practice

See Overview, pages 11–12.
Recognition Tests:
A ● • •   B • ● •   C • • ●
1. departure [B]   6. everywhere [A]
2. announcement [B]   7. neighborhood [A]
3. passengers [A]   8. thirty-four [C]
4. souvenir [C]   9. tomorrow [B]
5. directions [B]   10. important [B]

A ● •   B • ●
1. sorry [A]   6. Europe [A]
2. tourist [A]   7. New York [B]
3. remain [B]   8. delay [B]
4. depart [B]   9. Paris [A]
5. alarm [B]   10. doctor [A]

Review stress patterns practiced earlier in the book. For example:

1. noun compounds (see under Conversation in this unit);

2. words with unstressed prefixes (*a-, de-, ex-,* etc.): alarm, attention, announcement; before, below; delay, depart, departure, department; example, excuse; important; pronounce; remain, repeat; tomorrow.

Diagnostic Test

The purpose of this test is to identify students' weaknesses in pronunciation, in order to determine which sounds need the most attention for a particular class or language group or for individual students. The test can also be used at the end of the course to check students' progress.

Each item in the "Shopping List" tests one or two sounds. For example:

Shopping List
1. some Chinese tea; some French cheese (Get the cheapest cheese, please.)

Result Sheet
1. iy (sheep)
   tʃ (chair)

The Result Sheet indicates that in item 1 the teacher should listen for the sounds iy (as in *sheep*) and tʃ (as in *chair*), and evaluate student performance in these. The sound iy occurs here in the words *Chinese, tea, cheese, cheapest,* and *please*; the sound tʃ occurs in the words *Chinese, French, cheese,* and *cheapest*.

Administering the Test

Prepare a copy of the written test for the student(s). The test can be used in two alternative forms, depending on the level of the class. It can be photocopied and given to students as it appears here, or a version suitable for less advanced students can be prepared by omitting the material in parentheses. If necessary, students at a more elementary level can be asked to repeat the items rather than read them.

The test can be given to the whole class together if the students share the same native language. Ask a number of students to read each test item and record an average of the results. If the class is of mixed nationalities, the test can be given to groups of students or to individuals. It is a good idea to tape-record students' performances, if possible. Otherwise, students can be asked to repeat an item as many times as necessary for the teacher to record the results.

Since errors in pronunciation are often due to confusion caused by spelling, it is advisable to check errors by saying the mispronounced words correctly and asking the student to repeat them.

Suggested symbols for grading
√ = no difficulty with this sound
x√ = minor difficulty
x = moderate difficulty
xx = extreme difficulty

Test

Shopping List

1. some Chinese tea; some French cheese (Get the cheapest cheese, please).
2. six fish; fifty little shrimp (Make sure the fish are fresh.)
3. ten eggs for breakfast (Get big eggs.)
4. eight small paper plates; six steaks (Let's make them for supper on Saturday.)
5. a jar of jam; apples and oranges; a cabbage
6. five pounds of veal (very good veal); some calves' liver (We'll have the liver this evening.)
7. nuts; honey; one dozen hot buns (or perhaps a half dozen)
8. some jars of jam (or maybe marmalade); a box of matches
9. some strong string; four long forks
10. some yellow onions; yogurt
11. a watch; a white wool sweater (a warm one)
12. some good cookies or chocolate cake; sugar; coffee; cream or milk
13. two soup spoons; paper plates; a new coffee cup; some fruit juice (possibly grape-fruit juice)
14. some lettuce and two tomatoes for a salad; a pound of bananas or other fruit
15. a leather belt for Mother; another sweater for Father
16. ice cream; white rice or fried rice (Maybe buy some fried rice at the Chinese restaurant.)
17. some toys for the boys (maybe a blue ball for Bob)
18. nine lemons; a pound of brown onions; some flowers for the house
19. a dozen cans of New Zealand peas, please (or get frozen peas)
20. a girl's shirt; a purse; a skirt (to wear to work)
21. cold drinks; some good bread for dinner
22. a bottle of olive oil; a leg of lamb (to broil for lunch); apples and melons, please
23. something for Mr. Smith (It's his birthday on Thursday.)
24. four or five beers; half a pound of pears; four chairs for the party tomorrow
25. a television; some measuring tape

Result Sheet

1. iy   (sheep)   _____

   tʃ   (chair)   _____

2. ɪ   (ship)   _____

   ʃ   (shoe)   _____

3. ɛ   (yes)   _____

   g   (girl)   _____

4. ey   (train)   _____

   s   (sun)   _____

5. æ   (hat)   _____

   dʒ   (joke)   _____

6. v   (van)   _____

7. ʌ   (cup)   _____

   h   (hat)   _____

8. ɑ   (father)   _____

   m   (mouth)   _____

9. ɔ   (ball)   _____

   ŋ   (ring)   _____

10. ow   (no)   _____

    y   (yellow)   _____

11. w   (window)   _____

12. ʊ   (book)   _____

    k   (key)   _____

13. uw   (boot)   _____

    p   (pen)   _____

14. ə   (a banana)   _____

    t   (tie)   _____

15. ər   (letter)   _____

    ð   (the feather)   _____

16. ay   (fine)   _____

    r   (rain)   _____

17. ɔy   (boy)   _____

    b   (baby)   _____

18. aw   (house)   _____

    n   (nose)   _____

19. z   (zoo)   _____

20. ɜr   (word)   _____

21. d   (door)   _____

22. l   (letter, ball)   _____

23. θ   (think)   _____

24. r after vowels (here, there)   _____

    f   (fan)   _____

25. ʒ   (television)   _____

List of Likely Errors

This is an index of errors commonly made and sounds found difficult by speakers of different languages or language groups.* References are shown to units in the Student's Book providing practice in features of stress and intonation. Practice of individual sounds can be located using the table of contents.

Arabic

Vowels

Meaning is carried chiefly by consonants in Arabic; all English vowels may need practice.
A glottal stop is often added before vowels at the beginning of words.

ɪ (ship):	confused with ɛ (yes)
ʌ (cup):	confused with æ (hat) or ɑ (father)
ey (train):	confused with ɛ (yes) or ay (fine)
ɔ (ball),	
ow (no):	pronounced too short; may be confused with each other or with ʌ (cup) or ɑ (father)
ɜr (word)	
ɔy (boy):	confused with ay (fine)
ə (a banana)	

Consonants

Silent consonants often pronounced.
Consonants in general may sound overemphasized.
Difficulty with groups of consonants, especially groups of three or more consonants; vowels often inserted between the consonants.

p:	confused with b
v:	pronounced f, or sometimes b
g:	may be confused with k or dʒ (joke)
θ (think):	usually pronounced t (though the sound θ exists in classical Arabic)
ð (feather):	usually pronounced d (though the sound ð exists in classical Arabic)
ŋ (ring):	pronounced ŋg, ŋk, or ng
r:	trilled; vowels before r confused
h:	pronounced as a harsh sound
ʒ (television):	may be confused with ʃ (shoe), z, or dʒ (joke)
tʃ (chair):	may be pronounced ʃ (shoe)

*This list is adapted from the List of Likely Errors compiled by Sally Mellersh in *Introducing English Pronunciation* by Ann Baker, published by Cambridge University Press, 1982.

Stress, intonation, and rhythm

May sound abrupt, commanding. Too many syllables are stressed.
Word stress: Units 2, 8, 15, 19, 22, 29
Reduced vowels; weak forms: Units 8, 14, 19
Sentence rhythm: Units 5, 8, 13, 16, 17, 19, 25, 26, 39, 46
Joining words: Units 27, 28, 29
Rising intonation (and almost all intonation exercises): Units 1, 3, 4, 12, 44

Chinese

Vowels

Almost all vowels will need practice. Variation of vowel length (for example, lengthening stressed vowels before a voiced consonant) causes difficulty.

ɪ (ship):	confused with iy (sheep)
ɛ (yes):	confused with æ (hat) or ʌ (cup)
æ (hat):	confused with ʌ (cup), ɛ (yes), or ɑ (father); may be nasalized
ʊ (book):	confused with uw (boot)
uw (boot):	may be pronounced like the vowel y in French *tu* or confused with ʊ (book)
ʌ (cup):	may be confused with ɑ (father)
ey (train):	confused with ɛ (yes)
ɔ (ball):	may be confused with ow (no) or ɑ (father)
ay (fine), ɔy (boy), aw (house):	pronounced too short; sometimes replaced by first vowel alone
ə (a banana):	may be pronounced with rounded lips; often pronounced as the vowel in the spelling
ɜr (word):	may be pronounced with rounded lips

Consonants

Difficulty with final consonants: may be dropped, especially after a diphthong, or a short vowel may be added at the end.
Great difficulty with groups of consonants: vowels often inserted between consonants in initial clusters, vowels added or consonants dropped in final clusters.

l:	confused with r; confused with n by some speakers
z:	usually replaced with s
dʒ (joke):	sounds close to tʃ (chair)
ʃ (shoe):	confused with s or may sound close to h, especially before iy (sheep) or ɪ (ship)
ʒ (television):	may be confused with ʃ (shoe), s, or z
v:	replaced with f or sometimes w
θ (think):	replaced with t, s, or f
ð (feather):	replaced with d or z
b, d, g:	may be pronounced p, t, k, especially at the end of words

h: may be pronounced harshly; confused with s or ʃ (shoe) before iy
                           (sheep) or ɪ (ship)
y: found difficult before the vowels iy or ɪ

Intonation

Difficulty with intonation patterns that extend over a phrase or sentence.
Intonation may sound monotonous or sing-song.
Difficulty with the use of pitch as an element of English stress.
Falling intonation: Units 1, 3, 7, 9, 20, 33, 35, 37, 44 (Almost all intonation
   exercises would be useful.)
Expressing emotion: Units 4, 9, 37, 40, 44

Stress and rhythm

Sounds staccato; too many syllables stressed.
Joining words: Units 27, 28, 29
Sentence rhythm: Units 5, 8, 13, 16, 17, 19, 25, 26, 39, 46
Reduced vowels; weak forms: Units 8, 14, 19
Surprise; contrastive stress: Units 10, 38

Czech and Polish

Vowels

æ (hat):   pronounced ɛ (yes) or confused with ʌ (cup)
iy (sheep):   confused with ɪ (ship)
ow (no):   confused with ʌ (cup) or ɔ (ball); pronounced too short
ʊ (book):   confused with uw (boot)
uw (boot):   may be pronounced close to ʊ (book) by Polish speakers
ə (a banana)

Consonants

w: pronounced v
θ (think)
ð (feather)
ŋ (ring)
z: pronounced s in final position
b, d, g: pronounced, respectively, p, t, k in final
                           position
v: pronounced f in final position
dʒ (joke):   pronounced tʃ (chair) in final position
r: trilled

Stress

Word stress (predictable in Czech and Polish, always falling on the same syllable):
   Units 2, 8, 15, 19, 22, 29
Reduced vowels: Units 8, 14, 19

Dutch

Vowels

æ (hat):	pronounced ɛ (yes)
ʌ (cup):	confused with ɑ (father), or pronounced close to the vowel of ɜr (word)
ɔ (ball):	confused with ɑ (father) or ow (no)
ɪ (ship):	may be pronounced close to iy (sheep) or more like ɛ (yes)
ʊ (book):	may be pronounced more like uw (boot) or close to ʌ (cup)
ɜr (word):	pronounced with the lips pushed forward and rounded
ɔy (boy):	second sound may be too long

Consonants

Voiced consonants (d, v, etc.) tend to be replaced with their voiceless equivalents (t, f, etc.) at the end of words.

w:	confused with v (w usually replaced with v), or an intermediate sound may be made for both
θ (think):	pronounced t or s
ð (feather):	pronounced d or z
g:	pronounced k or non-English sound x (Bach)
z:	pronounced s, especially in final position
v:	pronounced f, especially in final position
ʒ (television):	pronounced ʃ (shoe), especially in final position
dʒ (joke):	pronounced tʃ (chair) in final position; sometimes pronounced ʒ (television)
ʃ (shoe):	may be pronounced s in final position
tʃ (chair):	may be replaced with ʃ (shoe)
d:	pronounced t in final position
b:	pronounced p in final position
r:	pronounced too far back (uvular r) or trilled
l:	may be pronounced as dark l where English has clear l
ŋ:	may be confused with ŋk in final position; ŋg (finger) may be pronounced without the g sound

Intonation

Intonation may sound flat or monotonous.
Rising intonation: Units 1, 3, 4, 12, 44
Falling intonation: Units 1, 3, 7, 9, 20, 33, 35, 37, 44

Farsi (Iranians)

Vowels

All vowels need practice.

ɪ (ship):	sounds close to iy (sheep)
æ (hat):	pronounced close to ɛ (yes), or confused with ʌ (cup)

ʌ (cup):	sounds close to ɑ (father)
ə (a banana)	
ɜr (word):	often pronounced ɛr
ow (no):	confused with ɔ (ball)
ʊ (book):	confused with uw (boot)
ɛ (yes):	may be confused with ɪ (ship) or æ (hat)
ɔy (boy):	confused with ay (fine) or ɔ (ball)
aw (house):	may be confused with ɑ (father) or ow (no)

Consonants

Difficulty with groups of consonants, especially at the beginning of a word; a vowel like ɛ (yes) is added before or between consonants.

w:	confused with v
θ (think):	usually pronounced t
ð (feather)	
s + consonant:	found difficult at the beginning of a word
ŋ (ring):	pronounced ŋg or ng
r:	trilled or flapped r; vowels before r cause difficulty
l:	only clear l used

Stress and rhythm

Word stress (predictable in Farsi): Units 2, 8, 15, 19, 22, 29
Reduced vowels; weak forms: Units 8, 14, 19
Sentence rhythm: Units 5, 8, 13, 16, 17, 19, 25, 26, 39, 46
Joining consonant sounds: Units 27, 28, 29

Finnish

A tendency to pronounce words as they are spelled.

Vowels

æ (hat):	pronounced ɛ (yes)
ɜr (word)	
ə (a banana)	

Consonants

Final groups of consonants may cause difficulty.

w:	pronounced v
θ (think)	
ð (feather)	
g:	confused with k
b:	confused with p, especially in final position
f:	confused with v, especially in final position
z:	pronounced s or ts

ʒ (television):	pronounced s or ts
d:	confused with t, especially in final position
ʃ (shoe):	pronounced s or ts
tʃ (chair):	confused with ʃ (shoe)
dʒ (joke):	pronounced tʃ (chair) or y

Intonation

Intonation may sound choppy or monotonous; falling intonation may be added on
 words in the middle of a sentence.
Rising intonation: Units 1, 3, 4, 12, 44
Falling intonation: Units 1, 3, 7, 9, 20, 33, 35, 37, 44

French

Vowels

Vowels in French are generally shorter in length than in English. They are
 also often produced further forward in the mouth, and the muscles tend to
 be tenser.

ɪ (ship):	sounds close to iy (sheep)
ʌ (cup):	may be pronounced close to the vowel of ɜr (word) or confused with ɑ (father)
ey (train):	confused with ɛ (yes); pronounced too short
ʊ (book):	sounds close to uw (boot)
æ (hat):	confused with ʌ (cup), ɑ (father), or ɛ (yes)
ɔ (ball):	may be confused with ow (no), both being pronounced as a pure o sound
iy (sheep):	pronounced too short; confused with ɪ (ship)
ə (a banana)	
ɔy (boy):	may be pronounced as ɔ (ball)
ɜr (word):	may be pronounced with lips pushed forward and rounded
ay (fine):	second sound may be too strong
aw (house):	second sound may be too strong

Consonants

Vowels are generally not lengthened before final voiced consonants (e.g., g, d),
 creating confusion with corresponding voiceless consonants (e.g., k, t).

h:	omitted or put in the wrong place
θ (think):	often replaced with s
ð (feather):	often replaced with z
r:	pronounced too far back, as uvular r
tʃ (chair):	often pronounced ʃ (shoe)
dʒ (joke):	often pronounced ʒ (television)
ŋ (ring):	may be pronounced as a nasalized vowel, or replaced with other nasal sounds (e.g., a French palatal nasal sound)
t:	has a different quality in French (dental t)

| p, t, k: | not aspirated at the beginning of a word, which may cause confusion with b, d, g |
| l: | only clear l used; a full vowel may be added before syllabic l |

Intonation

May sound flat or monotonous, or may have abrupt (rather than gliding) changes in intonation, giving an impression of being overemphatic.
Falling intonation: Units 1, 3, 7, 9, 20, 33, 35, 37, 44
Questions: Units 1, 3, 4, 12, 20, 35, 44
Exclamations: Units 9, 37, 44
Surprise: Units 4, 10

Stress and rhythm

An area of great difficulty. Stress in French is predictable, falling on the last syllable of a word or phrase.
All syllables may sound as if they are stressed equally; unstressed syllables are not shortened or pronounced with reduced vowels.
Word stress: Units 2, 8, 15, 19, 22, 29
Reduced vowels; weak forms: Units 8, 14, 19
Sentence rhythm: Units 5, 8, 13, 16, 17, 19, 25, 26, 39, 46
Contrastive stress: Units 10, 38

German

Vowels

A glottal stop may be added before a stressed vowel, especially at the beginning of a word.
Vowel sounds in general are made with tenser muscles in German and with more movement of the lips.

æ (hat):	pronounced ɛ (yes)
ɔ (ball):	may be confused with ow (no) or may sound close to ʌ (cup)
ɜr (word):	pronounced with rounded lips
ə (a banana):	not used frequently enough; may have a different quality
ey (train):	may sound too short; may be confused with ɛ (yes)
aw (house):	has a different quality

Consonants

Consonants are often pronounced more emphatically in German.

w:	confused with v
θ (think):	pronounced s
ð (feather):	pronounced z
z:	pronounced s, especially in final position
b, d, g:	pronounced, respectively, p, t, k in final position
v:	pronounced f, especially in final position
ʒ (television):	may be pronounced ʃ (shoe)
dʒ (joke):	may be pronounced tʃ (chair) or confused with y (yellow)

ŋ (ring):	may be confused with ŋg or ŋk; g sound may be omitted in words with ŋg (finger)
r:	usually too far back (uvular r), or pronounced as a flap
s:	at the beginning of a word, may be pronounced z before a vowel or as ʃ (shoe) before a consonant
l:	only clear l used

Stress and intonation

May sound staccato (because of glottal stops).
May sound abrupt or commanding.
Some speakers tend to add rising tones on each word in a sentence. (Intonation varies, depending on where the speaker is from.)
Joining words: Units 27, 28, 29
Weak forms: Units 8, 14, 19
Falling intonation (some speakers): Units 1, 3, 7, 9, 20, 33, 35, 37, 44

Greek

A tendency to pronounce words as they are spelled.

Vowels

Fewer vowels in Greek. In general, vowels tend to be pronounced with less movement of the lips than in English.

iy (sheep):	pronounced too short; confused with ɪ (ship)
æ (hat):	confused with ɑ (father) or ɛ (yes)
ʌ (cup):	confused with ɑ (father) or æ (hat)
ə (a banana)	
ow (no):	pronounced too short; confused with ɔ (ball), ʌ (cup), or ɑ (father)
uw (boot):	confused with ʊ (book); pronounced too short
ɔ (ball):	may be confused with ow (no)
ey (train):	may be pronounced ɛ (yes) or confused with ay (fine)
3r (word):	often pronounced with ɛ (yes) as the vowel

Consonants

ʃ (shoe):	pronounced s
ʒ (television):	pronounced z
tʃ (chair):	pronounced ts
dʒ (joke):	pronounced dz
w:	may be pronounced gw or g
h:	pronounced as a harsh sound like the non-English x (Bach)
r:	trilled; vowels before r found difficult, with the vowel ɑ (father) sometimes added before the r
p, t, k:	not aspirated at the beginning of words and may sound close to b, d, g
g:	sometimes pronounced as a softer, non-English sound

s:	pronounced z before m (and other voiced consonants)
z:	in final position may be confused with s
ŋ (ring):	may be pronounced ŋg

Stress and intonation

All syllables tend to be the same length; unstressed vowels are not reduced.
Intonation may sound annoyed or brusque.
Reduced vowels; weak forms: Units 8, 14, 19
Word stress (Greek has one stressed syllable per word; secondary stress may be
   omitted): Units 2, 8, 15, 19, 22, 29
Falling intonation: Units 1, 3, 7, 9, 20, 33, 35, 37, 44
Questions (including tag questions): Units 1, 3, 4, 12, 20, 35, 44
Joining words: Units 27, 28, 29

Hebrew

Vowels

Meaning is carried by consonants in Hebrew. All vowels need practice.

æ (hat):	confused with ɛ (yes) or ʌ (cup)
iy (sheep):	pronounced too short; confused with ɪ (ship)
ə (a banana):	may be pronounced close to ɛ (yes) or as the vowel in the spelling (though Hebrew has the sound ə)
ɜr (word):	pronounced close to ɛr (very) or with the vowel in the spelling
ʌ (cup):	confused with ɑ (father)
ey (train):	pronounced too short; confused with ɛ (yes)
ow (no):	pronounced too short; confused with ʌ (cup)

Consonants

Difficulty with groups of consonants. Vowels inserted between consonants.

ð (feather)	
θ (think)	
r:	pronounced too far back (uvular r) or confused with w
w:	confused with r or v
dʒ (joke):	may be confused with ʃ (shoe), z, or other sounds
h:	may be omitted, or may be pronounced harshly
ŋ (ring):	may be confused with m or n
l:	has a different quality in Hebrew

Stress, intonation, and rhythm

Intonation may sound annoyed, irritable, or complaining.
Stress sounds too even.
Word stress: Units 2, 8, 15, 19, 22, 29
Sentence rhythm: Units 5, 8, 13, 16, 17, 19, 25, 26, 39, 46
Falling intonation: Units 1, 3, 7, 9, 20, 33, 35, 37, 44

Hungarian

Vowels

æ (hat):   pronounced close to ɛ (yes), or confused with ɑ (father)
ɪ (ship):   confused with iy (sheep)
ə (a banana)
ʌ (cup):   confused with ɑ (father), ɔ (ball), or other vowels
ɑ (father):   may be confused with ɔ (ball)
ʊ (book):   confused with uw (boot)
ey (train):   sounds close to ɛ (yes)

Consonants

w: pronounced v
θ (think)
ð (feather)
ŋ (ring):   pronounced ŋk or ŋg
dʒ (joke):   pronounced dy or tʃ (chair)

Note:

letter c: may be pronounced ts
letter j: may be pronounced y
letter s: may sometimes be pronounced ʃ (shoe) or z

Stress and intonation

Sounds a little flat.
Exclamations: Units 9, 37, 44
Surprise; contrastive stress: Units 4, 10, 38
Word stress: Units 2, 8, 15, 19, 22, 29

Indian languages (including Gujerati, Hindi, Urdu, Punjabi)

Vowels

Vowels may tend to sound too short.

æ (hat):   confused with ɛ (yes)
ɔ (ball):   confused with ɑ (father) or ʌ (cup)
ey (train):   confused with ɛ (yes)
ow (no):   may be confused with ɔ (ball), both being pronounced as a pure
                      vowel o
ɔy (boy):   may be pronounced as ay (fine)
ɜr (word)
ə (a banana)

Consonants

Difficulty with groups of consonants, especially at the beginning of a word.
An extra vowel may be added after final consonants.

w:	confused with v, or an intermediate sound may be used for both
θ (think):	pronounced close to t
ð (feather):	pronounced close to d
t:	pronounced with the tongue curled back
d:	pronounced with the tongue curled back
z:	sounds close to s, especially in final position; sometimes pronounced as dʒ (joke) or dz
ʒ (television):	may sound like z, ʃ (shoe), or y
ʃ (shoe):	may be confused with s
l:	found difficult at the end of a word; tendency for only clear l to be used
ŋ (ring):	often pronounced ŋg, especially between vowels
r:	often pronounced as a trill or tap; vowels before r are often confused
p, t, k:	often not aspirated at the beginning of a word and may sound close to b, d, g
f:	may be pronounced p

Intonation

Intonation may sound lilting or sing-song, with too many high or rising tones, especially in the middle of a sentence.
Falling intonation: Units 1, 3, 7, 9, 20, 33, 35, 37, 44 (and almost all intonation exercises)

Stress and rhythm

Stress generally sounds too even.
Sentence rhythm: Units 5, 8, 13, 16, 17, 19, 25, 26, 39, 46
Word stress (predictable in Indian languages): Units 2, 8, 15, 19, 22, 29
Reduced vowels; weak forms: Units 8, 14, 19

Italian

Vowels

ɪ (ship):	sounds close to iy (sheep)
æ (hat):	confused with ɛ (yes) or ɑ (father)
ʌ (cup):	confused with ɑ (father) or æ (hat)
ə (a banana)	
ɜr (word):	confused with ɔr (north) or other sounds
ʊ (book):	confused with uw (boot)
ow (no):	confused with ɔ (ball), both being pronounced as a pure vowel o; sometimes confused with ɑ (father)
ɛ (yes):	confused with ey (train)

ay (fine),
ɔy (boy),
aw (house):   second sound may be too strong

Consonants

A tendency to pronounce words as they are spelled.
Difficulty with some groups of consonants.
An extra vowel is often added after final consonants.

h:	omitted or put in the wrong place
θ (think):	often pronounced t
ð (feather):	often pronounced d
z:	may be pronounced s, especially at the end of words
s:	pronounced z before m, l, n
r:	trilled
ʒ (television):	may be pronounced dʒ (joke), ʃ (shoe), or zy
y:	sometimes confused with dʒ (joke)
ŋ (ring):	often replaced with ŋg or n
w:	may be replaced with v
p, t, k:	not aspirated at the beginning of a word; may sound, respectively, like b, d, g

Stress and rhythm

Unstressed syllables pronounced with full vowels; all syllables may seem to be given equal weight.
Difficulty with reduced vowels and weak forms.
Joining words (an extra vowel may be added at the end of a word): Units 27, 28, 29
Word stress: Units 2, 8, 15, 19, 22, 29
Sentence rhythm: Units 5, 8, 13, 16, 17, 19, 25, 26, 39, 46

Intonation

May sound choppy or too restricted in range.
Questions: Units 1, 3, 4, 12, 20, 35, 44
Falling intonation: Units 1, 3, 7, 9, 20, 33, 35, 37, 44
Surprise; contrast: Units 4, 10, 38
Exclamations: Units 9, 37, 44

Japanese

Vowels

Usually sound too short.

ɜr (word):	sounds close to ɑ (father)
ə (a banana):	pronounced ɑ (father) or as the vowel in the spelling
ɪ (ship):	sounds close to iy (sheep); in some words, may be pronounced as a whispered sound and appear to be dropped

æ (hat):	pronounced as ɑ (father) or ɛ (yes)
ʌ (cup):	confused with ɑ (father), æ (hat), or other vowels
ʊ (book):	confused with uw (boot) or other vowels; in some words, may be pronounced as a whispered sound and appear to be dropped
uw (boot):	has a different quality (the lips are not rounded)
ow (no):	confused with ɔ (ball), with both sounds being replaced by a pure vowel o
ey (train):	may sound close to ɛ (yes)
iy (sheep):	pronounced too short, causing confusion with ɪ (ship)

Consonants

Great difficulty with groups of consonants; vowels are added between consonants. Difficulty with final consonants; an extra vowel is often added after the consonant, or the consonant may be dropped.

l:	sounds close to r
f:	confused with h before vowels like ɔ (ball) or uw (boot)
θ (think)	
ð (feather)	
v:	sounds close to b
w:	found difficult before uw (boot) or ʊ (book); when spelled *wh* may be pronounced f
z:	may be pronounced as dʒ (joke) before iy (sheep) or ɪ (ship) or as dz before uw (boot) or ʊ (book)
r:	confused with l; vowels before r may be confused, or the sound ɑ (father) may be added to the vowel
h:	confused with ʃ (shoe) before iy (sheep) or ɪ (ship); confused with f before uw (boot)
ʒ (television):	pronounced dʒ (joke) or ʃ (shoe)
s:	may be pronounced ʃ (shoe) before iy (sheep) or ɪ (ship)
t:	may be pronounced tʃ (chair) before iy or ɪ; may be pronounced ts before uw (boot) or ʊ (book)
d:	may be pronounced dʒ (joke) before iy or ɪ; may be pronounced dz before uw or ʊ
y:	found difficult before ɪ (ship) or iy (sheep)
n:	pronounced indistinctly in final position, where it may be confused with m or ŋ (ring)

Stress, intonation, and rhythm

Sounds staccato; an extra vowel is often added at the end of a word.
All syllables may seem to have equal stress.
Contrastive stress; surprise: Units 4, 10, 38
Stress in noun compounds: Units 22, 25
Reduced vowels; weak forms: Units 8, 14, 19
Falling intonation: Units 1, 3, 7, 9, 20, 33, 35, 37, 44 (and almost all intonation exercises)
Sentence rhythm: Units 5, 8, 13, 16, 17, 19, 25, 26, 39, 46

Khmer (Kampucheans)

Vowels

ɪ (ship):	confused with iy (sheep)
ʊ (book):	confused with uw (boot)
ə (a banana):	pronounced as the vowel in the spelling
æ (hat):	confused with ʌ (cup) and ɛ (yes)
ɜr (word):	sounds close to ɔr (north)
ey (train):	confused with ɛ (yes)
ow (no):	confused with ɔ (ball)
ay (fine),	
ɔy (boy),	
aw (house):	final consonants may be dropped after diphthongs

Consonants

Great difficulty with groups of consonants, especially in final position; one or more
  consonants may be dropped.

z:	may sound like s
f:	found difficult, especially in final position
s:	may sound close to h
θ (think)	
ð (feather)	
v:	may be confused with w or may sound close to b
ʒ (television):	confused with dʒ (joke)
ʃ (shoe):	confused with tʃ (chair)
dʒ (joke):	may be pronounced tʃ (chair) in final position
y:	may sound like dʒ (joke)
tʃ (chair):	may sound like t in final position
l:	confused with r after k or g

Stress and rhythm

Sound staccato.
Joining words: Units 27, 28, 29

Intonation

Falling intonation: Units 1, 3, 7, 9, 20, 33, 35, 37, 44 (and all intonation exercises)
Expressing emotion: Units 4, 9, 37, 40, 44

Portuguese

Vowels

Vowels may be nasalized before m, n, or ŋ (ring).
At the end of a word, unstressed vowels may seem to be dropped.

ɪ (ship):	sounds close to iy (sheep)
æ (hat):	confused with ɛ (yes) or ɑ (father)
ʊ (book):	confused with uw (boot)
ʌ (cup):	confused with æ (hat) or ɑ (father)
ɔ (ball):	may be confused with ɑ (father) or ʌ (cup)
ə (a banana):	found difficult especially by Brazilians
ow (no):	may sound close to ɔ (ball)

Consonants

Difficulty with groups of consonants; vowels often inserted before or between the consonants.

Final consonants dropped or not pronounced clearly.

r:	pronounced too far back or as a flap or trill; at the beginning of a word may sound close to h; vowels before r found difficult
h:	sometimes omitted, or added in the wrong place
θ (think)	
ð (feather)	
tʃ (chair):	pronounced ʃ (shoe)
dʒ (joke):	pronounced ʒ (television)
b:	may sound close to v
v:	may sound close to b in initial position
y:	sometimes omitted
z:	confused with s or ʒ (television), especially at the end of words
s + consonant:	found difficult, especially at the beginning of a word
n, m,	
ŋ (ring):	confused in final position, or may be pronounced as nasalized vowels
t:	may sound close to tʃ (chair) before iy (sheep) or ɪ (ship)
d:	may sound close to dʒ (joke) before iy or ɪ; may sound close to ð (feather) in the middle of a word
l:	in final position or before a consonant may be replaced with a vowel

Stress, intonation, and rhythm

Word stress: Units 2, 8, 15, 19, 22, 29

Stress in noun compounds: Units 22, 25

Sentence rhythm (especially speakers of Brazilian Portuguese): Units 5, 8, 13, 16, 17, 19, 25, 26, 39, 46

Reduced vowels; weak forms (especially speakers of Brazilian Portuguese): Units 8, 14, 19

Joining sounds: Units 27, 28, 29

Tag questions: Unit 20

Falling intonation: Units 1, 3, 7, 9, 20, 33, 35, 37, 44

Russian

Vowels

Vowels may sound too short, especially where they should be lengthened (in final position or before a voiced consonant).

æ (hat):	pronounced ɛ (yes)
ɜr (word):	pronounced as ɛr, ɔr (north), or with the vowel in the spelling
iy (sheep):	confused with ɪ (ship)
uw (boot):	confused with ʊ (book)
ɔ (ball):	confused with ow (no)
ey (train):	confused with ɛ (yes)
ɑ (father):	may sound close to wɑ in some words
ay (fine),	
ɔy (boy),	
aw (house):	second sound may be too strong
ə (a banana):	may be pronounced as the vowel in the spelling (though the sound ə exists in Russian)

Consonants

A tendency to pronounce consonants as soft, palatalized sounds before some vowels (like iy and ɛ).

θ (think)	
ð (feather)	
w:	confused with v
r:	trill or flap used
ŋ (ring):	pronounced n, ŋk, ŋg, or g
z:	pronounced s in final position
b, d, g:	pronounced, respectively, p, t, k in final position
v:	pronounced f in final position
h:	pronounced as a harsher, non-English sound x (Bach)
p, t, k:	not aspirated at the beginning of a word and may sound close to b, d, g
l:	clear l may be substituted for dark l, or dark l for clear l

Note:

Because of the Cyrillic alphabet:
letter B may be pronounced v
letter C may be pronounced s
letter P may be pronounced r
letter H may be pronounced n
letter g may be pronounced d

Intonation

What is considered to be neutral, unemotional intonation in Russian and English often differs. Intonation may sound impatient, unfriendly, bored, or overemotional in some types of sentences.

Yes/no questions: Unit 3
Statements: Units 3, 35
Tag questions: Unit 20
Alternative questions: Units 1, 27

Stress

Secondary stress in words is often omitted.
Word stress: Units 2, 8, 15, 19, 22, 29
Reduced forms: Units 8, 14, 19

Scandinavian languages: Swedish, Norwegian, Danish

Vowels

ɪ (ship):	sounds close to iy (sheep)
ʌ (cup):	may be pronounced close to ɑ (father) or with the lips rounded and further forward
ow (no):	may be replaced with uw (boot) or aw (house), or confused with ɔ (ball)
æ (hat):	confused with ɛ (yes) by some speakers
uw (boot):	may have a different quality
ʊ (book):	confused with uw (boot) or other vowels
ɜr (word):	may be said with the lips pushed forward and rounded
ey (train):	second part too long; sound may have a different quality
ay (fine),	
ɔy (boy):	second part too long
ə (a banana):	may not be quiet enough; not used frequently enough

Consonants

Swedes and Norwegians may make consonants spelled with doubled letters too
   long.

θ (think)	
ð (feather)	
w:	sounds close to v
dʒ (joke):	confused with y or pronounced dy
z:	pronounced s
ʒ (television):	sounds close to ʃ (shoe)
tʃ (chair):	confused with ʃ (shoe) or pronounced ty
r:	pronounced too far back (Danish) or trilled (Swedish, Norwegian)
b, d, g:	pronounced by Danes as p, t, k in final position

Stress and intonation

Statements may sound like questions; sentences may sound incomplete.
Unstressed syllables are often said with a high pitch.
Intonation may have a sing-song quality.

Falling intonation: Units 1, 3, 7, 9, 20, 33, 35, 37, 44 (and almost all intonation exercises)

Weak forms: Units 8, 14, 19

Serbo-Croatian

Vowels

ɪ (ship):	confused with iy (sheep)
æ (hat):	pronounced ɛ (yes) or confused with ʌ (cup)
3r (word):	confused with ɔr (north) or pronounced with the vowel in the spelling
ə (a banana):	pronounced as the vowel in the spelling
ʌ (cup):	confused with ɑ (father)
ʊ (book):	confused with uw (boot)
ow (no):	confused with ɔ (ball)

Consonants

w:	pronounced v
θ (think)	
ð (feather)	
ŋ (ring):	pronounced ŋg or ŋk
r:	trilled; difficulty with vowels before r

See note on Cyrillic alphabet, under Russian.

Spanish

A strong tendency to pronounce words as they are spelled.

Vowels

Vowels may sound too short, especially where they should be lengthened, as before a voiced consonant.

ɪ (ship):	confused with iy (sheep)
æ (hat):	confused with ɑ (father) or ʌ (cup)
ə (a banana):	pronounced as the vowel in the spelling
3r (word):	pronounced as it is spelled
ʌ (cup):	pronounced close to ɑ (father) or ɔ (ball)
ʊ (book):	confused with uw (boot)
ow (no):	confused with ɔ (ball), both being pronounced as a pure vowel o
ɔ (ball):	may be confused with ow or pronounced close to ɑ (father) or ʌ (cup)
iy (sheep):	pronounced too short; confused with ɪ (ship)

ε (yes):   confused with ey (train)
ay (fine),
ɔy (boy),
aw (house):   second sound may be too long

Consonants

Difficulty with groups of consonants; one or more consonants often dropped.
Final consonants dropped or not pronounced clearly.
Voiced consonants may be pronounced as voiceless at the end of words.

v:	pronounced b at the beginning of a word
h:	pronounced harshly, like the non-English sound x (Bach)
y:	confused with dʒ (joke)
ʃ (shoe):	pronounced tʃ (chair); confused by some speakers with s
z:	usually pronounced s
w:	sometimes pronounced b, gw, or g; found difficult especially before uw (boot) or ʊ (book)
d:	confused with ð (feather): d may sound like ð, especially in the middle of a word; ð may sound like d at the beginning of a word
m, n, ŋ (ring):	in final position, may be confused with each other or pronounced indistinctly
r:	flapped or strongly trilled; vowels before r found difficult
b:	may sound close to v, especially in the middle of a word
s + consonant:	often preceded by a vowel at the beginning of a word
s:	may be pronounced z before voiced consonants like m; may be replaced by h by some Latin Americans
p, t, k:	not aspirated at the beginning of a word and may sound close to b, d, g
g:	may have a softer sound in the middle of a word
ʒ (television):	found difficult by some speakers
θ (think):	found difficult, except by Castilian speakers
dʒ (joke):	may be confused with y or replaced by tʃ (chair)
l:	only clear l used

Stress, intonation, and rhythm

Stressed and unstressed syllables do not sound clearly distinguished; stress and
 rhythm too even, with all syllables about the same length.
Unstressed vowels are not reduced.
Sentence rhythm: Units 5, 8, 13, 16, 17, 19, 25, 26, 39, 46
Reduced vowels; weak forms: Units 8, 14, 19
Contrastive stress; surprise: Units 4, 10, 38
Stress in noun compounds: Units 22, 25
Word stress: Units 2, 8, 15, 19, 22, 29

Thai and Lao

Vowels

Vowels may be nasalized after h, m, or n.
A strong tendency to insert a glottal stop before vowels at the beginning of a
    word.

ʊ (book):	confused with uw (boot)
ɑ (father):	confused with ʌ (cup)
æ (hat):	confused with ɛ (yes) or ʌ (cup), or made too long
ey (train)	
ow (no)	
ay (fine)	
ɔy (boy)	

Consonants

Final consonants may be dropped, especially after diphthongs.
t may be substituted for other final consonants.
Great difficulty with groups of consonants, especially in final position, where one
    or more may be dropped.
In initial clusters, a short vowel is often inserted between consonants or a
    consonant may be dropped.

r:	confused with l
l:	confused with n in final position
θ (think)	
ð (feather)	
v:	confused with w; may be pronounced b in the middle of a word
z:	often pronounced s
ʒ (television):	confused with ʃ (shoe) or z
dʒ (joke):	pronounced tʃ (chair)
ʃ (shoe):	may be pronounced tʃ (chair)
g:	may be pronounced k

Intonation

Thai is a tone language, and each syllable is pronounced with a set tone.
All intonation exercises will be useful.

Stress and rhythm

Sounds staccato. Rhythm is too even. Words are not connected smoothly.
Final syllable of words is often stressed.
Joining words: Units 27, 28, 29
Contrastive stress; surprise: Units 10, 38
Sentence rhythm: Units 5, 8, 13, 16, 17, 19, 25, 26, 39, 46
Reduced vowels: Units 8, 14, 19
Word stress: Units 2, 8, 15, 19, 22, 29

Turkish

A strong tendency to pronounce words as they are spelled.

Vowels

æ (hat):	confused with ɛ (yes)
ʌ (cup):	confused with æ (hat)
ɑ (father):	may sound close to ʌ (cup)
uw (boot):	confused with ʊ (book)
ey (train):	close to ɛ (yes)
ɔ (ball):	confused with ow (no)
iy (sheep):	may sound close to ɪ (ship)
ə (a banana)	

Consonants

Difficulty with groups of consonants, especially at the beginning of a word; extra
vowels are often inserted.

w:	confused with v
θ (think)	
ð (feather)	
ŋ (ring):	pronounced ŋg or ŋk
r:	pronounced as a tap or trill; may be voiceless at the end of words; vowels before r found difficult
z:	pronounced s in final position
b, d, g:	pronounced, respectively, p, t, k in final position
v:	may be pronounced w, or in final position f
dʒ (joke):	pronounced tʃ (chair) in final position
k, g:	may have a different, softer quality before iy (sheep) and ɪ (ship)
m, n:	may be pronounced indistinctly in final position

Stress and intonation

Wh-questions: Units 3, 35
Word stress: Units 2, 8, 15, 19, 22, 29
Reduced vowels; weak forms: Units 8, 14, 19

Vietnamese

Vowels

ɪ (ship):	confused with iy (sheep)
æ (hat):	confused with ʌ (cup) or ɛ (yes)
ʊ (book):	confused with uw (boot)
ɑ (father):	confused with ɔ (ball)
ɜr (word):	may sound close to ɔr (north)
ey (train)	
ow (no)	

Consonants

Great difficulty with groups of consonants, especially in the middle or at the end
of words; one or more consonants may be dropped.

Final consonants may be dropped, especially after diphthongs like ay (fine) and ɔy
(boy).

θ (think)
ð (feather)

z:	pronounced s, especially in final position
s:	may be confused with t in final position
f:	sounds close to p
b:	confused with p in final position
p:	may be pronounced b in initial position
d:	pronounced t in final position
l:	confused with n in final position
r:	may be pronounced z
dʒ (joke):	may be pronounced ʒ (television)
tʃ (chair):	may be confused with t or ʃ (shoe), especially in final position
ʃ (shoe):	may be confused with s or t
g:	may have a different sound (softer or more guttural)

Intonation

Each syllable in Vietnamese has its own set tone.

Falling intonation: Units 1, 3, 7, 9, 20, 33, 35, 37, 44 (All intonation exercises will
be useful.)

Surprise; contrast: Units 4, 10, 38

Stress and rhythm

Sounds staccato.
Joining words: Units 27, 28, 29
Sentence rhythm: Units 5, 8, 13, 16, 17, 19, 25, 26, 39, 46
Word stress: Units 2, 8, 15, 19, 22, 29
Stress in noun compounds: Units 22, 25
Reduced vowels: Units 8, 14, 19